# WOLV



John Pollard
Herefordshire, ... Oxford.

During the w... served with the King's African Rifles and was thus enabled to indulge a boyhood passion for birds and animals on a scale that only Africa can provide.

His books include *Adventure Begins in Kenya*, *Africa for Adventure*, *African Zooman* and *The Long Safari*.

*By the same author*

Adventure begins in Kenya
Africa for Adventure
African Zoo Man
The Long Safari

# Wolves and Werewolves

JOHN POLLARD

ROBERT HALE · LONDON

*First published in Great Britain 1964*
*First paperback edition 1991*

ISBN 0-7090-4388-0

Robert Hale Limited
Clerkenwell House
Clerkenwell Green
London EC1R 0HT



Printed in Great Britain by
St Edmundsbury Press Limited, Bury St Edmunds, Suffolk
Bound by WBC Limited

*For*
Peter, Judith, Caroline and Diana

ACKNOWLEDGEMENTS

I wish to thank the following who kindly gave permission for the use of material from works published by them:

George Allen & Unwin Ltd.: Helge Instad, *Nunamiut*.

George Bell & Sons Ltd.: Jacob Grimm, *Teutonic Mythology*.

Cambridge University Press: J. Ritchie, *Animal Life in Scotland*.

T. & T. Clark: Hastings' *Encyclopaedia of Religion and Ethics*.

Alex. Gardner Ltd.: R. S. Fittis, *Sports and Pastimes of Scotland*.

Longmans, Green & Co. Ltd.: J. G. Millais, *The Mammals of Great Britain*.

Macmillan & Co. Ltd.: Sir James Frazer, *The Golden Bough*.

John Murray Ltd.: Axel Munthe, *The Story of San Michele*.

John Murray Ltd.: E. B. Tylor, *Primitive Culture*.

Routledge & Kegan Paul Ltd.: J. E. Harting, *Extinct British Animals*.

Martin Secker & Warburg Ltd.: Norman Douglas, *Siren Land*.

*Country Life:* Letter by John Corbett.

*The Field:* Roy MacGregor-Hastie, "Ambush for Wolves." R. I. Pocock, "Some Interesting Mediaeval Relics." Wlodek Puchalski, "Marauders in the Snow." Letters and articles by various authorities including Dugald Macintyre, Lieut.-Col. J. A. McQueen, Sir Hugh Rankin and Frank Wallace.

*The Guardian:* S. H. Moore: "Wolves in France." Reports on wolves in Europe.

*The Observer:* Dr. L. Harrison Matthews: "Wolf at the Door."
*Sunday Express:* "Man in Pit with Wolf."
*The Times:* Recent reports on wolves in Europe.
*The Irish Naturalist's Journal:* W. H. Workman: "The Wolf (Canis Lupus) in Ireland."
Professional Projects Ltd., proprietors of *Pulse.*
*The New Daily.*

I owe a special debt of gratitude to Madame Alberte Cadet who has generously permitted me to draw freely on her learned and fascinating article *"Les Loups en Charente"* (*Mémoires de la Société Archéologique et Historique de la Charente,* 1961) and also for some important unpublished matter; to Monsieur Ernest Vincent of Limoges for permission to use the material collected in his series of important articles *"Les Loups," Chronique Historique*; to Monsieur Manain Marc, Professeur au Collège de Châlus, Haute-Vienne for his kindness in referring me to important information; to Monsieur de Larambergue, Professeur de Zoologie, Université de Poitiers, for important recent notices about wolves in Vienne; and finally, and not least, to Mr. Colin Matheson, Keeper of Zoology in the National Museum of Wales, whose notable monograph *Changes in the Fauna of Wales within Historic Times* and article "The Grey Wolf" (*Antiquity,* 1943) have, together with the wealth of authorities quoted, proved of inestimable value.

No book on wolves could, of course, afford to ignore the fundamental articles by le Commandant Gaziot, Monsieur Raymond Rollinat and Monsieur Alex Feuillée-Billot, and I am deeply grateful to Monsieur Coquillat, General Secretary of the Société Linnéenne de Lyon, the General Secretary of the Société Nationale de Protection de la Nature and the editor of *La Terre et La Vie* for permission to use material cited by them.

I am grateful too for information received by correspondence with Mr. S. H. Moore, Monsieur P. Jay, President of the Société Archéologique et Littéraire de Barbezieux,

Colonel Niall Rankin, Professor Durward L. Allen of Purdue University, Lafayette, Mr. Dacre Balsdon of Exeter College, Oxford, and Mr. Raymond Hook of Nanyuki, and also for important references brought to my notice by Mrs. Marjorie Holt and Mrs. Hugh Gattie. Mr. Dafydd Wynn Parry kindly translated the extract from *Cantref Meirionydd* by Robert Prys Morris.

The following kindly supplied photographs, or gave permission for reproduction: Wlodek Puchalski, Esq., nos. 1, 2, 11, 12, 13 and 14; Monsieur P. Jay, 3; *The Field*, 4; The National Museum of Wales, 5; A. P. Kitchin, Esq., 6; Mme. Alberte Cadet, 7, 8, 9 and 10; and Professional Projects Limited, 15.

My debts are many, and I hope that any inadvertent omissions may be excused.

J.P.

# CONTENTS

# PREFACE

WOLVES are headline news. Every winter the clubman scanning the paper gets a vicarious thrill when he reads that packs are out in Italy or Spain, and have even been reported from France. France indeed has probably suffered more from wolves than any other country, not excluding Russia, and many horrors have been enacted there during the past hundred years. It is long since the cry "Wolf!" has been heard in Britain. Yet Ireland was known as "Wolfland" during the eighteenth century, and as recently as 1743 a wolf killed two children in Scotland.

Throughout the ages total warfare has been waged by man on his ancient enemy. Yet despite all his efforts the wolf fights back, sometimes with fearful fury. This book is concerned with the ruthless battle which still goes on today.

*Chapter One*

# The Wolves that Ate the Postman

FEBRUARY is a grim month in the Abruzzi, for then the mountain peaks are cloaked with ice, and the forest tracks are hidden under a thick carpet of snow. But in 1956 the falls had been the heaviest within living memory, and the long narrow valleys were cut off from the outside world. Avalanches had brought even the trains to a halt, and relief columns were sent out from the neighbouring towns with food and blankets for the freezing passengers. Yet snow or no snow, cold or no cold, the mail had to get through.

"There's talk of *lupi*," the post-master warned, as he slung the bag of letters and parcels across to his waiting colleague. "The driver of the Rome express reported seeing a pack near Monte Cassino. Of course they could have been dogs."

"*Lupi*—pah!" the *corriere* spat contemptuously. "The moment we have a bit of snow everyone starts talking about wolves. As long as I've got this," he flourished the heavy walking-stick meaningly, "and this," the knife gleamed red in the glow of the office fire, "no wolf shall prevent the *corriere* from performing his duty."

"Bravo!" the other grinned ironically. "Who knows, perhaps the government will award you a medal if you do get through, or a posthumous one if you don't!"

"Medal—pah!" the *corriere* rejoined. "Now if that's the lot I'll be off."

Outside in the street it had started snowing again, and the icy wind pierced even the thick army great-coat which the *corriere* was wearing. Cursing softly, he pulled on his gloves and tilted his peak cap to keep the flakes out of his eyes. He paused for a minute to gaze up the slope towards the distant farms. But nothing was visible in the blizzard except a clump of tall pines which seemed to beckon like ghostly sentinels at the forest's edge. Still the *corriere* wasn't worried. He had once boasted that he could have found his way to the farms blindfold. But that had been in summer. Now with daylight fading and the track masked by fresh snow he began for the first time in his life to feel unsure of his direction. The further he advanced into the forest the less certain he became, and after stumbling for a kilometre among the trees he suddenly realized with a sense of mounting panic that he was well and truly lost. Cursing loudly he switched on his torch with the intention of returning in his tracks, but already they were filled with snow, and the best he could do was to plod straight on. On should have meant going downhill towards the village, but he had an unpleasant sensation that he was still ascending. Angrily he turned about, only to find that he was climbing again. In desperation he set off to a flank in the hope that he might hit the track. Instead he found himself lost in the forest maze, alone in the night. Just then a faint howl was borne on the wind, and as he struggled on it grew louder and closer. His first reaction was one of relief. The farms, as he knew to his cost, kept powerful watch-dogs, so it seemed at last that he was approaching his destination. Then he remembered that the farm dogs greeted strangers with a furious baying. Only one beast howled in the Abruzzi at night.

As his torch-beam cut the darkness like a lighthouse in a storm it reflected six pairs of eyes gleaming in the darkness; green eyes set slantwise, the eyes of hunting wolves. The *corriere* ran blindly, following the torch-beam, dropping the bag of letters as he tripped over a fallen bough. Before he could recover it a grey shape leaped straight at him, striking out with its fore-paws at his unprotected face. It was the big dog-wolf showing the way to its hunger-pinched family howling in a circle behind. Lashing out with his stick, and cursing madly, the *corriere* felt in his pocket and drew his knife. But even as the wolf retreated startled, its mate rushed in and knocked the man over. That was the end. Next day a search party found all that remained of his body not far from the abandoned sack.

Such tragedies are by no means unique in the Abruzzi. Six years before, in 1950, a soldier set out to spend his leave at home. The way lay across the mountains as the village where he lived stood at the head of a remote valley, far from a main road. But the soldier was not deterred by this. Being a countryman he was familiar with the route, while his army training had inured him to long marches over rough ground. Besides, the prospect of a trek across the hills in the chill autumn air, with a royal homecoming at the end of it, filled him with an anticipatory glow. He waved a cheerful farewell to his comrades as he left the train at a wayside station, and turned into the *ristorante* for refreshment before his journey. When the proprietor learned his destination he shook his head forebodingly.

"It's a long step," he warned. "Best part of twenty kilometres. But I suppose being a *soldato* you've got a gun."

"Never fear," the young man grinned, affectionately patting his musket. "And I've a sharp *bajonetta* too if I meet any brigands."

"I wasn't thinking of brigands," the other mused. "I was thinking of *lupi*."

"Wolves," the soldier scoffed. "There won't be any of those about until the snow comes at Christmas."

"Don't you be too sure," the *trattore* pursued. "Only yesterday Rocco here lost two sheep."

"It is true," the shepherd nodded. "Two of my best sheep, too, and my neighbour has lost a cow."

"Sheep! Cows! What has this to do with me?" the youth laughed. "Don't you worry, *amici*. If I see a wolf I shall shoot him dead with my trusty *moschetto*. But I must be off, or I shan't reach home by nightfall."

As he strode up the track beside the forest the soldier's

thoughts were gay and carefree. What a surprise his old father and mother would have when he walked in. He smiled to himself as he imagined the look of incredulous joy on their wizened features. What celebrations there would be that evening when the neighbours came in to welcome him home, and his father, as he always did on such occasions, broached a new cask of wine! Then too there was Fioretta, the prettiest girl in the valley, they all said. She had promised to marry him if he came home safe from the army, and hadn't already acquired a wife. How she had teased him when they were last together, strolling in the April moonlight up the village street. Oh, yes, Fioretta would be there to welcome him, and her brother Jacobino, his boyhood friend, and all her other brothers and sisters, and her mother and father, the woodman, and all their relations. In fact the whole village would turn out to greet him on his return.

The track wound upwards and the scenery became wilder, and soon he had left the pine-woods and was out on the open moors. As he gained the col that separated the valley he had just ascended from the one which led to the village a rain squall blew up from the south. The soldier buttoned his greatcoat more firmly at the neck, pulled down his cap tighter, and adjusted the strap of his heavy pack. Just then his eye caught a movement in the mist, like that of the shadow cast by a large dog. A dog meant shepherds and, although it was surprising to find them still up in the mountains so late in the year, their presence was doubly welcome. He shouted a cheery hail, but the words were lost in the rain and wind. Just then he saw the dog again, only this time much closer. Come to think of it, it looked too large for a shepherd dog, and much more like a wolf. A wolf! Why hadn't he thought of it before? This must be one of the brutes that had worried Rocco's sheep, and eaten his neighbour's cow. Well, it wouldn't eat any more sheep or cows, he reflected grimly, clasping the butt of his gun. But before he could unsling it the wolf leaped straight at his throat. He was hurled to the ground by the impact and threw up his arms to protect his face. Suddenly he remembered the bayonet at his side and drew it from its sheath. By now the wolf had him firmly by the neck. He managed to stab it with the bayonet again and again but it would not loosen its grip, and it eventually died with its teeth still sunk deep in his neck.

"With his last reserves of strength," as *The Times* correspondent so graphically described the incident, "the soldier began dragging himself and the dead wolf towards his home. He was found dead this morning, still gripped by the wolf, and a long trail of blood showed how far he had been able to struggle with the weight of the wolf before collapsing."

Four years later in the mountains near Perugia, close to Lake Trasimene where Hannibal defeated the Romans, a woodcutter was busy felling trees. The season was Christmas, and such as imagine that Italy is a land of winter warmth and sunshine would have been speedily disillusioned by the heavy falls of snow. The snow was accompanied by a severe frost, and the woodman blew on his hands as he left his warm cabin to continue his task. His way lay up through the forest to a small clearing, and as he slouched along, axe on shoulder, he wondered if the snow became much deeper whether he would be able to work at all. As he toiled up the track little beads of perspiration appeared on his handsome bearded face. Wiping them away he paused for a moment to glance back down the rise. As he did so a low growl made him swing round. Creeping up behind him was a large wolf with its teeth bared in a savage grin. Behind it stood another, its eyes glinting red in the sun. Both beasts were lean and emaciated, and hunger had clearly mastered their natural fear of man.

Still growling horribly, the big wolf leaped at the woodman's face, but he raised his axe in self defence and prepared to sell his life dearly. The heavy blade rebounded from the beast's thick skull as its leap was arrested in mid-flight. Following up his advantage the woodman struck the wolf a second blow across its arched back. Before it could recover he struck again right between the eyes. It lay stunned on the ground, and the man turned about to face its companion. It was fortunate that he did so, for maddened by the scent of blood it too plunged into the fray. The sheer fury of the charge brought the woodman to his knees, and the wolf's fangs met in his arm as he threw up the axe-haft to protect his face. Weakened by loss of blood he swung his axe in desperation. As luck would have it the blade landed square on the tip of his assailant's nose, and with a mournful howl the wolf ran back to the forest. As the woodman wiped the blood from his eyes the first wolf's body began to stir. Before the beast could recover he cut off its head, and so ended its treacherous life. The news of the struggle soon reached the village, and a posse of men and boys arrived to collect the wolf's carcase. They all carried guns as well as axes as this was the fourth wolf to have been killed in the district during the cold spell. It weighed eight stone even in its famished state, and in its prime must have been nearer ten.*

* It was reported from Rome on 18th November 1963, that a pack of wolves had entered a sheepfold in the Gran Sasso and killed 80 of the inmates.

*Chapter Two*

# Wolves at the Gates of Paris

UNTIL quite recently wolves constituted a greater menace in France than anywhere else in western Europe. The vast forests that covered the eastern and south-western districts from the Marne to the Pyrenees provided just the kind of cover that wolves require. They flourished too in Brittany and the Norman *bocage*, and were perhaps commonest of all in the Massif Central and the areas immediately adjacent to it. Only the Pas de Calais was free of them, and every winter they emerged from their retreats to attack the livestock near the hamlets and villages. Unfortunately they by no means confined their assaults to horses, goats, oxen and sheep, but killed and ate women and children as well. Indeed news of their presence spread panic among the local peasantry, whose resources were rarely adequate to combat their depredations. Only the nobles in their castles and the inhabitants of the larger towns remained safe from the wolves, though in times of stress and terror even cities suffered invasion, and on one memorable occasion the capital itself.

In 1439 Paris presented a very different appearance from what it does today. Outside the walls was a series of scattered communities divided by broad green meadows, while Montmartre was a wooded hill. More than 100,000 people were crowded along the banks of the Seine and about the Ile de la Cité, while shepherds grazed their flocks right up to the edge of the forest which flanked the outskirts.

The Hundred Years War had reduced France to sorry straits, and although the English invaders had been expelled from the eastern provinces, and the king had returned at last to Paris, a spirit of anarchy was abroad. Charles VII it was true had been reconciled to John the Fearless, the ruthless Duke of Burgundy, murderer of his father's brother, but his power depended ultimately on the Armagnac mercenaries who were the Burgundians' bitterest enemies. The result was continuous civil war waged openly in the city streets. The dread Ecorcheurs or, "Flayers", murdered and tortured the citizens at will. Old men and women were roasted for sport, while women were raped and their children butchered. The streets were filled with the victims' corpses, but no one dared to clear them away. Soon plagues broke out, and this coupled with the famine which the war and civil struggles had occasioned speedily decimated the populace as never before. It was perhaps the worst moment in history that Paris had ever known for the daily tale of scarcely credible barbarities surpassed even the worst excesses of the French Revolution. But a new terror was yet to come, and from a source which no one guessed.

Despite the plague and the anarchy the shepherds still camped in the open spaces, but neither they nor their savage dogs were prepared for the horde of grey invaders that slunk out of the forest when autumn fell. Like the majority of the larger carnivorous animals, wolves normally avoid human beings, but in times of war and famine they speedily overcome their innate fear, and once they have tasted human flesh they are rarely intimidated even by the presence of armed men. The troubles in Paris offered precisely the kind of circumstances that favour wolves, for in times of war and pestilence people are usually too occupied to pay much attention to wild predators. So the packs, attracted by the scent of dead and dying, soon boldly attacked the shepherds themselves. First, however, they killed the dogs which are rarely a match for a wolf on its own ground, and when the dogs were gone their masters were left with no means of warning of the beasts' insidious approach. For wolves move silently at night like shadows, and only dogs are sufficiently sensitive to detect their presence.

The shepherds were dragged from their bivouacs beside the watch-fires or surprised and eaten on their way to the city. Indeed, within the space of a single fortnight fourteen people perished in the area between Montmartre and the Porte Sainte-Antoine. When the news reached the citizens that Paris was ringed by wolves they trembled afresh, and rarely visited the outskirts by day, if they could help it, and never by night. Even the Écorcheurs temporarily ceased from their pillage now that the city was confronted with a foe even more terrible than they. For a time the Armagnacs and Burgundians observed a truce for mutual protection against the wolves whose boldness increased from hour to hour.

But in the end the wolves left Paris, though the fear that they might return continued to haunt the inhabitants. In fact they sometimes did appear in the forest of Fontainebleau, and even during the winter of 1963 considerable excitement was occasioned by a report that wolves had been seen in the district of the Haute-Marne. When times are hard, and Paris has known many hard times since 1439, the thoughts of her citizens instinctively return to a grim period when the howl of wolves was heard in the suburbs, and danger lurked among the thickets of Montmartre.

More than two hundred years later the ambitions of Louis XIV received a temporary set-back at the Peace of Ryswick. War had raged through Europe for twenty years and as there were none left to hunt them the wolves had flourished in the forests of France as never before. As usual the south and west had suffered worst from their raids, and the regions bounding the Loire had become dangerous both for the farmers and their stock. Orléans had become a fortress garrisoned by troops, but soon it was to become a refuge from the attacks of hungry wolves. The packs, rendered bold by success, turned on the local women and children, and soon instituted a reign of terror. When normal methods proved useless the magistrates arranged battues. These consisted of drives through wolf-infested country with army marksmen stationed at strategic points. Whenever a wolf attempted to break through the cordon it was swiftly accounted for, and in the end two hundred beasts were destroyed. Even a single wolf is capable of enormous damage, so that the alarm caused by so many may be readily imagined. Despite the battues, attacks on human beings continued with frightening persistence, until not even the soldiers themselves were safe. Many were chased right up to the city walls, and pulled down and killed before they could gain sanctuary. For months the toll mounted, and even as late as 1712 no less than a hundred people died in the forests about Orléans. Today such figures seem scarcely credible, and bear eloquent witness to the sheer scale of the wolf-menace in eighteenth-century France. Nor did it end then, but continued right through the following century into contemporary times. The loss in human life during the last two hundred years must prove shocking to all who examine the figures or investigate the many tragedies that have been recorded. Today France is probably rid of wolves, though only probably. Every winter wolves are reported, usually in error, but some accounts have gained credence. There have not, however, been any reports of attacks on human beings since World War I, and the tragedy of a little local Red Riding-hood has long been forgotten.

*Chapter Three*

# Little Red Ridinghood

THE story of Little Red Ridinghood is perhaps the best known of all nursery legends. Children hear it when they are not long out of their cradles, and the terror of it remains with them for the rest of their lives. The tale itself is agelessly old and occurs in one form or another in areas as far apart as France and China. It was probably told to Stone Age youngsters in the days when the howl of prehistoric wolves was only too familiar to the cave-dwellers huddling round the fire. Even today the tragedy of *Le Petit Chaperon Rouge* is sometimes repeated.

On the 26th January 1914 a pretty little eight-year-old was setting out for school. She was a farmer's daughter, and lived at La Coquille in Dordogne, the hilly inland district of south-west France where beasts other than harmless sometimes roamed. She turned briefly to wave her basket before entering the wood, and then her dainty form faded among the trees. As her parents returned to their tasks they little realized that they would never see their darling alive again.

Darkness was already closing in when the little girl came out of school and walked up the village street in the direction of the wood. Normally, despite the stories she had heard about elves and wicked fairies she did not fear the wood at all, but that evening the bare branches seemed laden with menace and for the first time in her life she felt afraid as she started on the dim forest track. A queer feeling that she was being watched made her quicken her step, and as she passed a black thicket she broke into a run. Suddenly a large dog-like creature silently materialized from among the bracken, and stood barring her way. The child paused, stirred by a nameless dread, for the "dog" had prick ears and a long curling brush. When it opened its lean muzzle in a brief coughing howl it revealed two rows of white teeth. Turning round she started to run back towards the village, but had only gone a few yards when the wolf leaped at her and bore her to the ground.

When their daughter failed to return at the usual hour her parents did not at first grow anxious. She sometimes stayed in the village to play with friends or to call on a relation. But when darkness fell and she had still not arrived her father set out for the village. When he reached the thicket a whitish object lying among the leaves immediately attracted his attention. As he directed the lantern beam more fully upon it he recognized his daughter's basket, and beyond some fragments of her clothing.

That wolves sometimes roamed in the vicinity of schools with the aim of attacking small children was demonstrated near the end of the last century at the village of La Chaise in Charente. As the master, Monsieur Poitou, entered to begin the morning's lesson a laggard pupil rushed in fairly bursting with excitement.

"*Eh bien*—why are you late?" the master demanded. "Did you forget to get up in time?"

"*Mais non, Monsieur,*" the child panted. "I've just passed a big wolf in the wood of Garenne!"

As the wood was only a short distance from the school the master armed himself with a stick and strolled down to investigate. But by then the wolf had disappeared.

Even teachers were not safe on occasion. During the winter of 1900 the mistress of a village school near Saint Yrieix in the lonely mountain region of Haute-Vienne dismissed her pupils as usual at half past three. When the last had gone she turned to clear up the room and rearrange the books and slates. A mysterious series of thumps on the door startled her out of her reverie. Imagining that one of the children had returned to collect a garment or basket she quickly released the latch; but even as she did so she realized with a thrill of horror that some heavy creature or creatures were pressing to get in. Before she could drop the latch again the pressure from without forced the door open, and the next instant a pack of hungry wolves were swarming into the room. Her shrieks of terror roused the village, but by the time the neighbours arrived with guns and picks the wretched woman was dead and already half eaten.

In 1918 the wolves of France were still thriving in the favourable conditions provided by war. As the men had gone to the front there was no one left to hunt or trap them, and they bred in profusion in the forest depths. During 1915 a woman was attacked while returning from market, but saved her life by hiding in a barn; while between 1916 and 1918 no fewer than twenty-eight wolves were killed in the province of Marne, driven west it was supposed by the heavy shelling, and further south in Haute-Saône. Then in 1918 a second tragedy added authenticity to the Red Ridinghood legend. An old feeble-minded woman lived alone near the village of La Chapelle-Montbrandeix, some ten miles from Châlus in Haute-Vienne. Wolves had formerly been common in this province, but by then were accounted of rare occurrence. Once a week she left her cottage on the forest edge and came down to the village to purchase her few meagre provisions. Then for several weeks she failed to appear. It was the rain, some said, which had swollen the mountain streams and cut her off from the outside world. Perhaps she was ill still others suggested or, who knew, even dead. Someone really ought to go and inquire what had happened, but in fact, as usual, nobody did. Finally the weather cleared and a search party eventually set out from the village. The way was long, but the weather was mild, and they soon glimpsed the cottage ahead. No smoke was coming from the chimney, and there was a deserted air about it which raised their forebodings afresh. Manifestly the old woman had died. Then one of the boys who had strayed from the party ran back to announce that he had found a piece of red linen. His father recognized it as having belonged to the woman and asked where he had found it. They had scarcely reached the spot when a sudden cry made them all turn round in the opposite direction. A few yards away near the forest verge, not far from the stream where the woman drew her water, lay a pile of mangled clothing. There were traces of blood on the sward, and someone discovered a piece of skull.

"But what could have happened to her?" a big peasant inquired aghast. "Surely she could not have been murdered by some miserable assassins?"

"Assassins indeed," his companion nodded grimly. "The grey assassins of the forest."

"Holy Mother!" the giant breathed, crossing himself in horror. "Old Marthe has been killed and eaten by wolves."

In former times attacks by wolves were of notorious frequency in France, and sometimes took place quite openly before a watching crowd. One day a young girl of nine called Marie Vérité was leading a religious procession when a wolf suddenly sprang at her and carried her off. It was pursued by a band of three hundred armed persons, led by the marquis mounted on a mule. Yet despite every effort to circumvent it the wolf got away with its helpless victim and dragged her into the forest to eat. The story soon arose that it was in reality a werewolf which could change itself into man or beast at will. And so a guard went off with a supply of ammunition to have it blessed by the local prior. In the end he succeeded in tracking the beast, and surprised it sitting outside its lair. His shot proved mortal but the dying howls of the stricken wolf so affected his nerves that he died of fright.

A man-eating wolf once haunted the Cévennes and caused a reign of terror among the women and children. Its habit was to stalk lonely travellers and to pull them down and kill them before help could arrive. However, success engendered boldness and it was not very long before it began to attack grown men. Unfortunately for itself it reverted to sheep and was done to death by a party of shepherds.

Some years later a reaper was attacked by a wolf in the

Côte d'Or, but was lucky to escape with a bite on his hand. Later the wolf turned on a boy guarding cattle, and although a hunt was arranged it was never captured or destroyed. Earlier still a postman, a profession with an unfortunate history where wolves are concerned, was surprised by a wolf in the Bois de Vendresse in the Ardennes, but succeeded in escaping. The wolves in this area were believed to be reinforced by invasions from the Carpathians and possibly even further east and their attacks were correspondingly formidable. In Indre, a region formerly much favoured by wolves, a she-wolf, which had attacked some horses, wounded a man who had gone to the rescue of the boy in charge, but was subsequently accounted for.

In Lozère wolves attacked an elderly man who was saved by some foresters, while more recently a man and woman were pursued by a pack of three wolves. The man defended himself with a stick, but the woman who had fainted was severely bitten and subsequently died.

Today wolves are extinct in Brittany, but during the last century they abounded and were hunted both by local sportsmen and visitors from England. During one severe winter a little girl was attacked by a wolf in a barn on her father's farm in Morbihan. When the farmer returned from the fields that evening he surprised the animal at its kill. It immediately flew at him and knocked him down and he was lucky to escape with his life.

Indre was the scene of an even more alarming adventure. An elderly farmer of robust physique lived with his wife close by the village of La Tuilerie du Luzeret. One night he heard a disturbance in the enclosure where he kept his ducks. At the same time his watch-dog set up a furious barking, which soon changed to a note of distress. The farmer rose from his bed, opened the door-leaf and saw a wolf in the act of choking the dog. His shout diverted the beast's attention, and dropping the dog it charged furiously at the closed half of the door. Bursting it open it knocked the farmer over and bit him so severely that his clothes were badly torn. His wife, meantime, was rendered helpless by terror and refused to leave the bed. However her husband's grave predicament roused her from her trance, and she picked up a chopper which happened to be lying on the floor. Following his shouted instructions as he grappled with the wolf the woman struck the beast with all her strength across its fearsome head. When he felt the wolf weakening the farmer regained his feet, snatched the axe from his wife and killed it with a blow. He was by now in ill shape and collapsed in a faint while his wife hurried to the village to get help. The local doctor was abed, but dressed immediately and galloped to the farm on his horse. He found the room looking like a shambles, but the farmer was still alive. Despite the injuries he had sustained the tough old peasant recovered his health, and continued for many years to entertain his neighbours with thrilling accounts of the night's adventures.

*Chapter Four*

# "Candles" Burning in the Night

THE savage gleam of a wolf's eyes is a perennial feature that is frequently remarked upon, and usually likened by French observers to "candles burning in the night". Now a candle burns with an orange-coloured flame, and it is a curious circumstance that light reflected from a wild beast's eyes should so often be described as red and fiery. Something probably depends on the circumstance, for as with birds of prey the pupil tends to dilate and shimmer under the stimulus of anger or excitement. Again the type of light that a beast's eyes reflect obviously affects their colour. So the eyes of a pack of wolves prowling in the moonlight would appear to the observer to be as green as those of a lion or tiger, whereas the pupils of a hungry lurking animal reflected by a lamp or lantern might well seem to glow. On such occasions it is not difficult to understand how the wolf becomes a nightmare creature, and in the heated imagination of the terrified beholder the near living embodiment of a beast from hell. It is then that it may be relied upon to live up to its nature, and to show no mercy whether to beast, man, woman or helpless child.

One night in Charente a farmer and his wife left their home by the forest of Quatrevaux in order to attend a ball. On their return some hours later they were greeted to their alarm by a frantic uproar. The watch-dog, it seemed, had taken leave of its senses and was mounted on a straw-stack barking for all its worth. They were naturally at a loss to account for its behaviour, and wondered whether thieves had broken into the house. When it resolutely refused to descend despite all their coaxing they began to get angry and threatened it with a stick. Then suddenly the farmer observed two "candles" smouldering balefully near the bottom of the heap.

*"Tiens!"* he warned hoarsely, gripping his wife's arm. "There's a wolf in the farmyard after the dog!" By waving their arms and shouting they succeeded in driving the beast away, and rescuing the dog from its place of refuge. They both then retired to the safety of the house and bolted the door against the invader. They had not been in bed long when a tremendous din roused them from their slumbers. The wolf it seemed had returned for the dog, which was howling and scratching at the door. Under the pressure the door gave way, and the noise increased in volume. As the farmer feverishly groped for the matches to light the candle beside the bed the dog's frightened yelps were almost drowned by the crash of falling pans and crocks as pursued and pursuer hurtled round the room. When the tallow finally sputtered into flame the wife shrieked in terror at the awful vision that met her eyes, for the wolf was standing panting on the table gazing in baffled fury at the dog cowering beneath the bed. Once again the unhappy pair managed to drive the wolf away with shouts and threats, and eventually succeeded in restoring peace. But the cunning marauder was not to be denied, for it returned some nights later after the household had retired and killed and ate its unfortunate victim.

The partiality of wolves for dogs is notorious, though it seems strange that they should prefer to make a meal of one of their own kind, and one moreover most capable of resistance. But few dogs are a match for a grown wolf, and such as brave an encounter are swiftly despatched. Shortly before the First World War a terrified dog took refuge in a neighbour's farm and disappeared whimpering under the bed. After all attempts to dislodge it had failed the farmer went out to see what had frightened it. When he reached the gate barring entrance to the farmyard he glimpsed two "candles" burning by the hedge. It was now clear what had happened. The wolf had pursued the dog as far as the gate, but had failed to squeeze under the lower bar. His cry, *"Au loup!"* soon roused the neighbours who quickly locked up their own dogs in safety, and stalled their sheep and cattle for the night. Next day they set out to hunt the wolf, but it had returned to the forest and was far away.

A vision of wolves pursuing sleighs or carriages is usually associated with Russia or Poland. It comes therefore as something of a shock to learn that during the severe winter of 1870 wolves came out of the forest of La Braconne in Charente, and followed the farmers' waggons and traps. One night a farmer's wife was returning from a visit to some relations accompanied by her parents and child, when she suddenly noticed four "candles" burning in the darkness, reflected by the carriage lamps. Next moment two hungry wolves were bounding alongside the terrified pony, snapping at its flanks and howling dismally. The maddened creature broke into a gallop which threatened to upset the trap and leave the stranded occupants to the mercy of the wolves, but fortunately the driver retained her head and succeeded despite several kilometres of nightmare driving in delivering her family safe at the farm.

Subsequently wolves became so common that they ceased to occasion undue alarm, and during the summer it became their habit to follow the vehicles returning from the fairs and markets in the hope of tit-bits. The farmers then foolishly encouraged their boldness by deliberately dropping fragments of bread and meat in order to amuse their children. Little did they realize that in behaving in this fashion they were imperilling their own safety by accustoming the beasts to human beings.

An exciting incident involving a vehicle occurred about the turn of the century in the commune of Chasseneuil in Charente near the village of Chez-Burgaud. Two workmen were returning home by trap one evening by a road which passed through the forest of Bel-Air. They were approaching a cross-roads just as night was falling, when the elder, who was familiar with the phenomenon in question, suddenly noticed a pair of "candles" burning in the middle of the highway.

"Hullo—here's a wolf!" he remarked to his startled young companion, and cracked the whip hard against the rails. The beast however declined to be so easily intimidated, and the "candles" continued to smoulder as the trap passed by. For the first time the horse scented danger, and shied so violently that the passengers nearly fell out. A couple of hundred yards ahead two further "candles" were burning. This was too much for the horse. After swerving away it set off at a pace which no driver could hope to control. Whenever the terrified workmen turned round they could see the pairs of "candles" following, and coming closer every minute. A farm loomed out of the darkness and as they careered past it they heard the wolves howling behind. The hideous sound was so loud and near that it seemed to shake the forest, and so thoroughly unnerved the younger man that he shook like a leaf. In fact, as he later confessed to his family, he didn't recover his senses until they arrived in the town of Les Pins.

Wolves are possessed of preternatural cunning which surpasses even that of the fox. Being always on the look out for the weak or unprotected, they will haunt a place or district for days on end until a suitable opportunity of attacking occurs. Normally they will not take risks, except when emboldened by hunger or encouraged by success. On the whole they fear men, and prefer to try conclusions with women or children or the old and weakly of either sex. Yet not even grown men are exempt from danger when travelling in lonely places far removed from human aid. For a wolf has a sixth sense about such as cannot resist it, and as it is a master of camouflage and always moves in the shadow its presence is seldom detected until it is too late. It likes to take its victim off his guard, and then to knock him over with a blow from its forepaws so as to have him at its mercy as he lies helpless on the ground. But wolves are not only to be expected in the forest, for they keep a watchful eye on lonely habitations, and in particular on such occasions as when the master is away.

One winter's day a farmer set out for Blois, leaving his wife and small son alone. As the weather was fine the wife decided to put their pet sheep out to graze, though it was normally kept peasant fashion within the house. But instead of cropping the dewy sward the sheep bleated in terror and refused to leave its mistress. Annoyed by its insistence the woman attempted to drive it away, but it only pressed the closer. At that moment her son announced that he could see a large dog squatting by the hedge, so assuming that it had occasioned the sheep's alarm she permitted the trembling *mouton* to return indoors. Sometime later the farmer returned and his wife immediately told him what had happened. To her alarm he revealed that he had himself observed a beast "with eyes blazing like candles" crouching near the stable wall. He too had made the mistake of assuming that it was a dog, but now it was evident that it was a wolf after the sheep. The alarm was given, and next morning a battue was organized by the local farmers in the hope of destroying the beast. But though it was driven from cover it succeeded in escaping and was not seen again in that part of the country. The wolf had obviously watched the farmer leaving, and having no fear of women or children had lurked in the yard waiting for the sheep.

That wolves will stalk lonely travellers has already been remarked on and is well illustrated by the tale of the man who was given a bag of pork. It was dark when he left his parents' house, where they had recently killed a pig, and he had not gone far when he noticed the gleam of eyes reflected in the moonlight. At first he imagined that they belonged to a dog, and then as the "candles" grew in number he realized that a pack of wolves had scented the meat. Before he could summon help the hungry beasts leaped at the bag and tore it from him scattering the contents on the road. But even when the pork was eaten the scent still clung to him, and the wolves continued to follow him right up to his door.

Hearing his cries for help his wife ran out with a loaded pistol. By then the leaders were hard on his trail, and he succeeded in despatching two of them at point blank range.

Yet another traveller returning at night from the town of Saint Félix was only preserved from disaster by the wolf's fear of fire. He was carrying a lantern and as he passed a certain wood he remarked two pairs of "candles" reflected in the shadows. Realizing that he was being stalked by wolves and that if he had the misfortune to slip or stumble he would be immediately attacked, he hit on the stratagem of walking backwards and keeping the wolves at bay by directing the light-beam at their eyes. To cover several kilometres in this fashion with the constant chance of a third wolf creeping up behind demanded a degree of resolution of which few would have been capable. But by this simple ruse he succeeded in outwitting his cunning enemies, and eventually arrived safe at his cottage.

But wolves do not always attack at night, and many a lonely individual is doomed by day.

*Chapter Five*

# Murder in the Forest

ONE August during the middle of last century a considerable stir was caused in the commune of Mouzon in Charente when a man employed as a body-guard by a certain rich widow suddenly and mysteriously disappeared. The guard was a local inhabitant and well known in the neighbourhood which rendered his absence more baffling still. Yet despite a thorough search and the prolonged interrogation of his friends and relations no trace of the missing servant could be found. It was precisely, as the familiar cliché has it, as though he had dissolved into thin air. His aged mistress was the person most worried by his non-appearance, because she had come to depend on his advice and active assistance over a considerable number of years. That he should have simply packed up and left her was quite unthinkable particularly as she was reputed to have left him a considerable sum of money in her will. Besides he had left everything behind, apart from the clothes he was actually wearing, which was hardly the action of one who had decided to decamp.

Soon dark rumours were afloat. The man had robbed his mistress and absconded to Paris or abroad, or she herself had done away with him after he had rejected her advances. At this point a grisly discovery lent colour to the murder charge. One morning a forester felling trees on the estate noticed some blood on the ground. At first he supposed that some beast had been wounded, possibly by a poacher after deer. Then he found some clumps of hair among the bracken, which had the appearance of belonging to a man. When he reported his find the police were called in and at once the aspect of the case considerably darkened. Not only did the hair turn out to be human, but it was recognized at once as belonging to the missing man. Nevertheless to everyone's disappointment the *Sûreté* steadfastly declined to accuse the old lady, but persisted in seeking a motive elsewhere. A week passed, yet no light had been shed on the matter, and it began to appear as if the crime would never be solved. The trouble was, of course, that in the absence of a body there was no certainty that a crime had actually been committed, though the blood-stains and hair were hard to explain away. If the unfortunate man had been attacked by robbers, as some suggested, where had they hidden him and why had they first torn out chunks of his hair? Then someone wandering in the forest of Champlarnier happened to light on a half-eaten corpse. Enough clothes remained to identify the victim, and the melancholy truth was revealed that he had been eaten by wolves. The hungry pack, it seemed, had surprised him strolling in a copse, and then after killing him had dragged his body several kilometres. This it had done seemingly in accordance with the wolf's instinct to consume a victim near its lair. The villagers were as stunned by the news as if the old lady had confessed to being the murderess, for although several wolves had been reported on occasion in the district they had never been known previously to attack human beings.

The following year in an adjacent commune an even more shocking tragedy came to light. One chill autumn evening a buxom young peasant girl had crept stealthily out of her parents' cottage. She had the furtive aspect of a hunted creature and as she glanced up and down in desperation her pretty face contorted with a spasm of pain. Making up her mind she turned down the hill in the direction of the neighbouring wood. Arrived at the outskirts she paused for an instant to see whether anyone was following before slipping like a shadow among the trees.

Some days later a forester's widow happened to be passing through the wood in question when her attention was attracted by an object lying among the leaves. It proved to her horror to be the mangled trunk of a newborn baby whose head and limbs had been devoured by wolves. Clearly the child had been recently exposed by its mother in an attempt to conceal its birth, and as it lay in the forest the savage beasts had heard its helpless cries.

Hungry wolves will often follow travellers even in broad daylight, as a lawyer's clerk discovered on the road to Jurignac. He was carrying a satchel containing a brief, which his master wanted delivered by hand. The road was little frequented, but as he passed a wood he had an uncanny sensation that he was being followed. Soon the feeling became so irresistible that he was obliged to turn round though no one ever appeared. The possibility that a thief had seen the satchel and decided to steal it in the belief that it contained a sum of money gave him considerable unease, yet how anyone could stalk him and yet remain invisible was a mystery indeed. Just as he had begun to suspect that it was all a trick of the imagination he glimpsed a lean shape slinking in the shadow of the trees. Panic stricken by the knowledge that he was being trailed by a wolf the youth's first reaction was to run for his life. But to run would, of course, have betrayed his fear and encouraged the attack he was so anxious to avoid. So he contented himself by quickening his pace in the somewhat vain hope that he might out-distance his pursuer. But the faster he walked the nearer the wolf approached, and even when he could not see it he could feel its cruel eyes watching him from every copse and hedge. How long he could have resisted the temptation to flee he never learned for just at that moment he entered the outskirts of the town. Half-crazed by the experience he collapsed in the notary's office babbling in terror and laughing by turns.

About the same time an insurance agent was travelling in the vicinity of Les Pins. The country was wild and forested, and as his clients were widely dispersed through the area he made frequent long journeys to lonely spots. When he mentioned the "large dogs" which often kept pace with him whenever he happened to pass a wood the farmers' faces turned grave. Those weren't dogs, they warned, but savage wolves. Or worse, wild wolf-dog crosses that were a menace alike to man and beast. His employers should provide him with a trap or a horse before it was too late, otherwise one day he would be reported missing, and discovered in the forest minus his head. But the agent who had become quite used by then to having wolves as his companions only smiled grimly and proceeded on his way.

Towards the close of the century a landowner set out to inspect the woods in the neighbourhood of Taponnat and La Rochefoucauld. At a spot known as Les Reclous a wolf suddenly appeared, and followed him along the road to Classeneuil. Whenever the beast came too close to be pleasant the alarmed *propriétaire* waved his stick. But each time he turned his back on it it quickly regained lost ground. The drama of the situation is not hard to visualize by anyone who has had the misfortune to be stalked by a dog. But a dog even at its most hostile is rarely a killer animal, while a wolf at its best is still a fierce wild beast. In this instance the wolf evidently sized up its quarry and decided that he would not be likely to succumb without a hard fight. At any rate it eventually retired from the scene leaving the *propriétaire* much shaken but happily unscathed.

The persistence shown by wolves in marking down their victims is well illustrated by another adventure in Charente. A youth happened to be walking near a forest when, like the lawyer's clerk, he sensed the presence of an unseen watcher. As he continued on his journey he became increasingly conscious that he was being followed although it was long before he finally glimpsed the wolf. Fortunately he saw a farm-house at that moment, and earnestly begged the owner to grant him sanctuary inside. When he emerged sometime later it was only to discover that the wolf had by no means abandoned its quest. Indeed it still continued to stalk him cat-like in the shadows until the terror of the situation made the hair prickle on his neck. At length he reached a hamlet not far from his destination where a second wolf materialized and joined in the pursuit. It, like the first, kept at a safe distance until he was out in the open, and then swiftly and surely closed the gap. The wretched youth gave himself up for lost, but for some reason or other the beasts failed to attack. Nevertheless the menace of their presence all but rendered him demented, and the horror of the experience remained with him all his days.

Curiously enough the young man's grandmother chanced to be watching her sheep in a meadow close by. Suddenly a wolf slunk out of the forest and seized a fat ewe before her startled eyes. By dint of using its muzzle and tail in concert it slowly forced its victim back towards the trees. However the cry *"Au loup!"* quickly roused the neighbouring peasants who ran to the rescue waving sticks and pitch-forks. When the wolf realized that it was surrounded it eviscerated the ewe in anger before furiously dashing it on the ground. Only then did it return to the shelter of the wood.

But it was not always domestic animals that required protection from their keepers. Sometimes indeed it was the other way round.

One summer morning a lad called Bouyer was guarding a horse and two oxen near a wood. While passing the time looking for mushrooms in a neighbouring copse he suddenly saw a wolf. As the beasts were at that time plentiful in the neighbourhood he was not unduly alarmed, but when he waved his stick at it and shouted "Wolf!" the animal suddenly charged. If the wolf had expected an easy meal it was rapidly disillusioned, for the boy struck out to such purpose with his clenched fists that to begin with it retired. However it soon returned to the attack, whereupon the valiant *gamin* seized the animal by its furry throat and pushed with all his strength. Though by this manœuvre he succeeded in protecting his face he received severe bites on his wrists and fingers, and was eventually forced to the ground. The battle started anew with the wolf snapping and tugging in an effort to release its head while the child hung on like grim death. But the odds were too heavy and soon the boy must have succumbed through loss of blood had not the oxen come to his rescue. Lowering their heads they advanced in a solid phalanx in a gallant attempt to save their little master. Intimidated by the novelty of the attack the wolf withdrew for a short distance and gave vent to its anger by tearing up the ground. The boy called to the oxen which stationed themselves over him, so that he sat protected beneath their horns. The wolf ran off and the faithful creatures licked the boy's bleeding wounds.

Dogs too could prove as faithful, although wolves frequently preyed on them and carried them off from the farms. One day a little girl was guarding her sheep in La Rochette when a wolf came out of the forest and seized a ewe. Her bitch at once attacked it and despite its mistress's anguished cries chased it back into the forest. But no dog is a match for a wolf on its own ground and needless to say it was never seen again.

The bravery of peasants whose beasts were attacked was correspondingly amazing, and particularly in the case of women who were naturally far more vulnerable than men. A young shepherdess called Cécile Pannetier from Charme in Charente was one day guarding her flock of sheep near the village. Suddenly a wolf appeared and pounced on a lamb. Before the ferocious beast could make off with its prey, the girl instead of running for her life valiantly grabbed it by its long bushy tail and rained blows on its back with her crook. Infuriated by this sturdy defence the wolf abandoned the lamb and attacked its protector. Fortunately at that moment a party of farmers roused by her cries arrived in time to save her.

On another occasion a certain Madame Calland was driving a mule-cart to fetch the potatoes which her husband and son were digging up in a field near a forest. As she reached some copses of young trees she saw an enormous wolf, thin with hunger, coming out of a vineyard beside the road. It leaped at once at the mule's head, but its mistress nothing daunted got down from the cart and beat it with a stick. The wolf at once abandoned the mule and turned on the woman, tearing her clothing. Hearing her cries for help her husband and son ran to her assistance, but when it saw them approaching the wolf ran off none the worse for its beating.

On at least two occasions encounters with wolves had an amusing sequel instead of ending in tragedy. During one severe winter several people noticed a lone wolf prowling about in the vicinity of Cognac. Sometimes it was seen at one point, sometimes at another, and then one day it boldly crossed the bridge over the river and made for the town. A man happened to be passing when this occurred, and attacked the wolf with his stick. Instead of running away the beast leaped at its tormentor and tore into pieces the basket he was carrying. Finally it took refuge in the adjacent park. The man gave the alarm and in due course the official wolf-hunter arrived with a pack of dogs. The wolf was driven from its hiding-place, trapped by the dogs against a wall, and finally captured alive. When it was all over the local wits praised the wolf's intelligence for preferring the enticing contents of the basket, which contained his lunch, to its old tough owner!

A story is also told about a musician who had been performing at a wedding, and returning at night through a wood, fell into a wolf-trap. To his horror he discovered that he was not alone, for two eyes were glowing fiercely in the darkness beside him, and he gave himself up for lost. Fortunately despite his fall he had managed to retain his hold on his fiddle, and decided to try out the soothing effects of music on his savage companion. To his relief the wolf seemed quite appalled by the eerie sound, and crouched whining in a corner. Next morning the trappers could scarcely believe their eyes when they lighted on their ill-sorted catch.

That it pays to take wolves seriously was shown when a charcoal-burner attempted to imitate their howls. Irritated by the mournful sound which had been echoing through the forest one January morning he took off one of his wooden sabots and by setting his lips to the opening produced a very tolerable imitation of a wolf's howl. Before he knew what had happened he found himself surrounded and was obliged to decamp to the shelter of his cabin. There he remained besieged until the pack finally removed to other quarters.

The great forest of La Braconne in Charente was famous for its deer, as the local poachers were only too well aware, and it was a common practice for them to station themselves at dawn at likely points where the herds were known to pass. One morning a man was lying up at a place where the tracks crossed in the forest in the hope of poaching a hind, but when none put in an appearance he soon fell asleep. He awoke with an overmastering impression that he was no longer alone. When he opened his eyes a lean wolf's muzzle was sniffing him over an inch from his nose. At first he was too horror-struck even to stir, but soon the instinct for self-preservation began to assert itself and he decided to leap up and yell for help. He was on the point of doing so when he suddenly realized that to summon the local foresters would merely be to exchange the frying-pan for the fire. There were laws against poaching, and he had no intention of spending the rest of his life in gaol. Better far to risk the wolf, which after all might be expected to show some fellow sympathy for a brother robber when in trouble. Suiting action to the thought the poacher leaped up cursing and waving his arms at the wolf. The beast was so startled by the unexpected movement that it trotted away without more ado.

The ancient superstition that if a wolf saw a man before the man saw the wolf he would be struck dumb with terror was proved by a traveller walking towards Angoulême one night. He became suddenly aware of two eyes blazing in the darkness, but before the wolf could attack him he had the presence of mind to hold out his hat. The beast immediately leaped at it and tore the lining, and while its attention was distracted the man escaped. When he attempted to summon help he discovered that the shock of the encounter had temporarily deprived him of speech.

The sudden appearance of a wolf had a similar effect on a shepherdess some years later. The girl was busy knitting when she happened to notice that the flock had gathered in alarm in the centre of the meadow. At the same instant she glimpsed a brown shadow gliding towards them and realized that they were being stalked by a wolf. She was so unnerved by the incident that she uttered no sound and remained rooted to the spot as the wolf seized her best ewe and dragged it off into the forest.

*Chapter Six*

# The Beast of the Gévaudan

GREAT though the terror caused by wolves in France was during the nineteenth and earlier centuries it paled into insignificance beside the grisly saga of the Beast of the Gévaudan. The Gévaudan is a wild mountain district in Lozère where wolves were formerly common and survive possibly to this day, but few now recall the grim tale of the man-eating wolf that spread fear through the region for upwards of two years. The incidents started with a normal type of wolf attack but ended in a massacre.

In June 1764 a woman was herding her cattle near Langogne, some twenty miles north-east of Mende, when a huge and ferocious wolf attacked her. The loyal oxen rallied to her rescue, and the wolf was driven off after tearing a part of her clothing. Though the latter event appeared to have no special significance at the time it was destined to produce the direst results, for it marked the wolf's first contact with a human being and its partial success soon encouraged it to attack again.

On the 3rd July a girl of fourteen was killed and partly eaten near the village of Habats, the first in a ghastly and perhaps unexampled toll of victims. Another girl was attacked and killed on the 8th August, and at the beginning of September two boys were slain and eaten by the same fierce beast. The method of attack was similar in each case. The wolf would deliver a frontal assault, knocking its victim down with a blow from its fore-paws, and savagely biting him in the face. Success increased its boldness, and on the 6th September it killed a grown woman. By the end of

October three more girls had died as well as two small children, and all had been mangled in hideous ways. Panic possessed the Gévaudan, and the inhabitants moved about in constant terror of their lives. There was a brief respite, possibly because the beast was mating, and then on 25th November an elderly woman was killed. This fresh outrage was speedily followed by others, and then again the attacker lay low. But at the end of the month it killed two children in Auvergne.

So great was the outcry that a detachment of dragoons was despatched from Clermont-Ferrand under the command of a Captain Duhamel with orders to destroy the beast. As its whereabouts were unknown a series of battues was arranged in the local forests in the hope of driving it into the open. These were pursued with such thoroughness that no less than seventy-four wolves were hunted and destroyed. Any hope that the killer had been included in their number was soon abandoned as on Christmas Eve a young boy was bitten to death and two days later a shepherd. Then on the 27th December the partially eaten remains of a girl of nineteen were found near Mende. At the end of the month yet another girl was killed in Rouergne, and by now the inhabitants, rendered frantic, were describing the animal as a werewolf or sorcerer or even as a bestial incarnation of the devil himself.

The Church could no longer ignore the challenge, and when on the 1st January the wolf started the new year with a trio of murders the Bishop of Mende ordered prayers to be said in public for the general safety. But the wolf proved as impervious to prayers as to hunting and the killings went on as before. On the 6th January two women were eaten in separate districts, and next day it was the turn of a girl.

On the 12th January seven children belonging to the village of Villaret were playing together when the ravening creature suddenly appeared and boldly seized the smallest. Instead of flying in panic the three biggest children bravely stood their ground, and actually put the wolf to flight, though not before it had bitten most of their playmates. Only a short time later it attacked and killed a boy of fifteen, and on the 15th January a girl of twenty was savagely done to death.

Up till this point the wolf, as is usually the case with this ferocious but essentially cowardly beast, had confined its attacks in the main to women and children. But on the 18th January it flew at three men, who were fortunately armed with pitch-forks and succeeded in driving it off. Their description of their assailant excited universal interest, as many conflicting rumours were current about the wolf. It was, they said, of enormous size, yet displayed the kind of agility that is more usually associated with a lion or tiger. Sometimes it reared up on its hind-legs like a bear, while at others it attacked from a horizontal position. This led to the doubt whether it was a wolf at all until someone remembered that only the latter was in the habit of removing its victims' heads.

On the 22nd January the wolf surprised and killed a young woman in the parish of Lorcière. Her body was discovered next day, terribly mangled and with the head, as usual, separated from the trunk. Before the local inhabitants could recover from the shock the beast seized a small child near Saugnes and carried it off to eat. Then before the month was out yet another innocent woman paid the penalty.

Had the wolf confined its activities to one specific area it might have been possible to corner it, but as its depredations ranged over forty leagues no one knew where it might next attack. So widespread was the alarm that 20,000 men took part in a notable drive. But though many wolves were killed, the man-eater remained as cunning as ever. On the 1st February it attacked a young man near Marvejols. His life was saved by his dog which forced the wolf to release its hold, but only after he had been severely wounded. On the 9th February it appeared once more in the Gévaudan and decapitated a young girl of fourteen.

By now the news of the terrible beast had reached Paris, and Louis XV ordered Monsieur Donneval, a famous hunter who had accounted for more than 1,200 wolves in Normandy, to proceed to the Gévaudan and rid the region of its pest. Donneval at once set out for the south with his son, taking with him his best pack of hounds. In the meantime the wolf had attacked another child which, though rescued by its mother, subsequently died. Then, as if to celebrate Saint Valentine, it killed and ate a woman and child in Auvergne, and bit two others so savagely that they were admitted to the hospital at Saint-Flous.

As the attacks had reached epidemic proportions all kinds of exaggerated reports began to circulate about the wolf. It was said by many to be as tall as a calf, of remarkable length and of a reddish hue with a brown streak running down its back. It was also said to herald its assaults by a cat-like twitching of its monstrous tail. It is again scarcely surprising to learn in the circumstances that its jaws emitted a fetid stench. In short it was generally believed to have been far larger and stronger than the average wolf with some highly unusual features.

The king set a price on its head, but despite every effort the killings continued. A small girl was eaten on the 24th February, and a woman in Auvergne on the 4th March. On the 8th the wolf ate a child of ten, and the following day it snatched another. The child's father forced it to abandon its victim, but was not in time to save its life. So savage and relentless had the creature now grown that it was rarely satisfied with a single killing, and on this occasion it attacked and ate a young woman in Auvergne the very next day. On the 11th March a child of five was snatched in the Gévaudan and eaten, and on a subsequent occasion it wounded a party of children as well as a grown man. A shepherd was next attacked as he guarded his sheep, but his life was saved by the heroic action of his cows. Next day the horrible news arrived that it had killed and decapitated yet another young woman, while on the 5th April it killed a young boy. Between the 7th April and the 24th May it killed and partially devoured a girl of seventeen, three children, a man and a woman.

Donneval meantime was scouring the district with his hounds, and by the 22nd May had accounted for a further nineteen wolves. But his success met with a chilly reception from the local inhabitants who were solely concerned with the fate of the man-eating beast. On the 28th May the wolf attacked a horseman on the road to Amorgne, but although the rider was dragged from the saddle by the fury of the assault he managed to save his life. On the 1st June, just one year after the original attacks had begun, the wolf killed and ate a little girl in Amorgne. Her companion escaped by climbing up some rocks, and was discovered three days later alive but demented. A third girl was killed during the same period, and another guarding a horse was knocked down by the beast's whirlwind charge. A rescue party arrived and drove the wolf off, but the girl had been bitten in the neck and died a few days later. A child of ten was more fortunate. The wolf's charge duly knocked her down, but the oxen she was guarding lowered their horns and saved her. Another little girl owed her life to her pigs, which kept the wolf at bay until her mother's arrival.

Even Louis was alarmed by the scale of the killings and summoned Antoine de Bauterre, his *lieutenant des chasses*, to Versailles and ordered him to leave for the Gévaudan and Auvergne with the best pack of wolf-hounds that he could muster. At his request several royal princes loaned their hounds and the lieutenant moved south at the head of an impressive retinue. On his arrival a fortnight later the Donnevals left for home their reputations as wolf-hunters sadly impaired.

Soon after Bauterre's arrival the wolf attacked an elderly woman while she sat spinning and watching her cattle. After biting her throat it ripped open her cheeks with its murderous paws and finally killed her. Her body was discovered by a small girl whose piercing shrieks drove the wolf from her carcase. By the middle of August two more children and a young girl had paid the penalty of living in Lozère, and during September three further children died. It was clear that the wolf now lived entirely off human beings, having once made the fatal discovery that they were simpler to kill than beasts.

On the 21st Antoine and his hunters disturbed an enormous wolf in the forests belonging to the nuns of the Abbé Royal. The lieutenant shot at the beast and wounded it, and it was subsequently seen to fall. But before the hounds could reach it it had regained its feet. It was then hit by a bullet fired by a certain Monsieur Rinchard who was stationed near Antoine, and it finally collapsed some distance away. The wolf proved to be the biggest that Antoine had ever seen, and weighed 130 *livres*, the better part of ten stone. Several people claimed to recognize it as the animal which had attacked them, and it was confidently believed that the man-killer had met its doom. The carcase was taken to Clermond-Ferrand where an autopsy was performed. As it lay on the table its eyes gleamed so hypnotically that even in death no one could withstand its gaze. It was also noted that the beast's tail was of extraordinary length, and these facts coupled with the discovery of some particles of red clothing in its belly seemed to confirm its identity with the Beast of the Gévaudan. But although the attacks ceased for a time and Antoine was duly rewarded some still remained unconvinced.

Then on the 10th December a youth was wounded, and by the end of the month two small girls had been killed and eaten. After this the attacks ceased again for a month, only to recur the following February. The killer, it was now clear, far from being destroyed, had merely lain up until the coast was clear of hunters. The next victim was a small neatherd, but his life was saved, as in previous instances, by the instinctive reaction of the cattle. On the 14th a woman was wounded, it was presumed by the same beast, and further battues were organized. These failed like their predecessors to discover the whereabouts of the man-eater, and on the 4th March a child was killed. Ten days later the beast grown bolder snatched a child of eight from near his home. When the child could not be found his father set out to search for him, and came upon his half-eaten remains a kilometre away.

Five days later the wolf attacked an old man, who was severely savaged but saved by a passer-by. Then a little girl was eaten.

For a space the attacks ceased, and it was high summer when they suddenly commenced again. A young girl guarding some sheep was killed and partly eaten, and a like fate befell another in a village some distance away. The Gévaudan, it was said, had become an accursed land where devils roamed abroad and devoured young children. It was a nightmare autumn, for beside many wounded, a youth, a woman and two more children died. Then during the spring of 1767 the killings recommenced. During March and April three children were killed and partly eaten.

Attempts were now made to destroy the wolf by laying out poisoned bait. But while fresh meat was available the beast studiously ignored all such crude attempts to entrap it. On the 17th April a girl was eaten, and so at the beginning of May, were another child and a middle-aged woman. Later another woman died and a number of children were eaten in the neighbourhood of Grèzes. Once again the Church took a hand, and prayers were offered everywhere on behalf of the stricken inhabitants.

Fresh battues were organized by the Marquis d'Apches, now that Antoine and his hounds had returned to Versailles. Then on the 19th June, just two years after the attacks had started, a posse of 300 hunters was assembled in the forest of la Ténazeire. One of these, a man of sixty called Jean Chastel, was posted near la Sogne-d'Auvert when a gigantic beast broke from cover. He killed it with his first shot, and upon examining the carcase was convinced that it was the man-killer. To begin with, it too was of a reddish hue, with a long tail and massive muzzle though its weight was only 109 pounds. When its stomach was opened it was found to contain the broken shoulder bone belonging to a girl who had been killed only twenty-four hours earlier.

The beast was stuffed and sent to Versailles to claim a reward from the king, but it unfortunately putrified in the summer heat, and Louis who by now was tired of the whole affair made fun of Chastel and ordered him to bury it. Nevertheless the old man's action did not go unrewarded by his fellow citizens, and a sum of money was collected in the diocese of Mende. That this wolf was in fact the man-killer was proved when the attacks ceased with its death and the Gévaudan awoke at last from its long nightmare.

What can be gleaned after an interval of two hundred years of this long and unparalleled tale of horror? Was in fact only one beast involved, or were there two or even more? That a single wolf could have succeeded in escaping such intensive battues as were organized to destroy it over a considerable period seems scarcely credible. If, on the other hand, two wolves were involved this might help to explain why the killing of the first failed to put an end to the outrages. If again the attacks were perpetrated by a pack then the majority may have been killed, while the survivors carried on the grisly business. Apart from its size there was no guarantee that Antoine's wolf was the beast in question, though the fact that the killings temporarily ceased might suggest that it had had a hand in them. A second wolf might then have lighted on the remains left by the first, and acquired like it a taste for human flesh. Whatever the truth of the matter the shooting of the second wolf certainly brought peace to the Gévaudan, though only at the end of much suffering. In all sixty people died, a ghastly record that was happily destined never to be approached again.

*Chapter Seven*

# Cry "Wolf!"

ONE of the most dreaded scourges that has afflicted mankind from time immemorial is rabies or hydrophobia, the hideous malady often culminating in death or madness which rabid animals transmit through the medium of a bite. Dogs are perhaps most susceptible to the disease, though other domestic animals can fall victims too, and the rigid laws of quarantine which are applied in Britain and elsewhere to all imported beasts were designed to prevent its spread. Until Pasteur isolated anthrax towards the end of last century and succeeded in producing a vaccine to combat rabies, no cure was known. So when people were bitten by rabid dogs, as frequently happened, more particularly in the east where pariah dogs were common, they usually died a horrible death.

Hundreds of dogs were inoculated with serum taken from rabid specimens in an attempt to discover an antidote, and hundreds inevitably died in the process as did many human victims. Pasteur reserved for himself the dangerous task of extracting the fatal saliva, and after many heartbreaking failures and the taking of appalling risks he finally obtained a cure.

The news spread abroad and reached the ears of the Czar who had had brought to his notice a terrible tragedy at Smolensk. More virulent far than the bite of a mad dog was that of a rabid wolf, and in countries where the wolf was found such attacks were usually fatal. In Smolensk six peasants had recently been bitten by a pack of mad wolves, and were terribly mauled about the face and hands. The Czar promptly sent them to Paris at his own expense in the hope that Pasteur could affect a cure. No one realized what little chance the peasants stood of retaining their lives or sanity better than Pasteur himself, for the reaction from the bite of an infected wolf was far more swift than that of a dog, and if received in the face was normally fatal. Undeterred, the great doctor endeavoured to do what he could for his screaming patients, isolating them in a special ward in charge of his friend Professor Tillaux, the most eminent surgeon in France. Once a day Pasteur in person inoculated them assisted by Axel Munthe who records the scene so graphically in *The Story of San Michele.*

On one occasion a burly patient in the last extremity of delirium, his eyes blazing fanatically and his mouth covered with froth, uttered a ghastly cry and attempted to leap out of bed. In the course of the struggle to keep him down Munthe narrowly escaped being bitten himself and so contracting the disease. The man died next day in appalling agony gazing steadfastly at the crucifix laid on his bed.

Within the space of three days all the peasants were raging in delirium, and howling in their madness like demented wolves. The horror of the scene unnerved many of the nurses who fled down the corridors away from the ghastly sound. Only Pasteur remained calm throughout the entire episode, stepping quietly from bed to bed as he ministered to the victims' needs. But in the end even his iron resolution gave way, and after a brief consultation with Tillaux the men were put painlessly to sleep.

During the eighteenth century attacks by rabid wolves were recorded from the Alpes-Maritimes. In those days the hinterland of the French Riviera was a wild and savage region, and the gaunt terrors of the forest often invaded the suburbs of Nice. One account is contained in a letter from a local physician to a medical acquaintance, recorded by Commandant Gaziot.

"Dear friend," it begins, "I should like to take this opportunity of informing you about a dreadful event that has happened here. The mayor of Nice appointed the commander of the National Guard to take charge of the operations against the wolves, and it was agreed that every citizen who produced a wolf's head should receive a reward of sixty francs. Well last week a wolf attacked an old woman at midday near the village, and after killing her ate her face. Some men ran to her assistance but at their approach the savage beast left the woman and tore their faces too. Meantime some armed people banded together to destroy the animal, but whenever one advanced it charged him viciously. Within an hour it had not only killed the woman, but had bitten and mangled the faces of seven men as well as that of the victim's daughter. Finally the last of these unfortunate people seeing the wolf leaping at him, its claws all set to tear his face, boldly seized it in his arms and hurled it to the ground. There with the assistance of the others it was finally despatched. After wreaking such carnage the conclusion is inescapable that this wolf was rabid, and that its wretched victims are faced with a like fate. In the meantime as a remedy for their wounds we are following the advice of Fossart, Liéland and others, and treating them with normal antiseptics mixed with mercury ointment. Moreover we stimulate sweating with diaphoretics, and give them light purges compound of sweet mercury and scammony. As the wounds, as I have stated, are mostly in the region of the head, while the cuts are deep, I do not dare to apply the mercury in conventional doses, but make greater use of antiseptics such as terebrinth and myrrh mixed with honey and the yolks of eggs. With regard to the diet, it consists of soup, orange drinks and burdock. Meanwhile we wait on events. We shall see later what will be the fate of these unfortunate people. You will appreciate only too well my anxiety in such circumstances for I am faced with maladies that I have never seen, and to combat which my medical experience is inadequate.

"I beg you, my dear sir, to acquaint me at once with the rule that I must follow, for I count on the continuance of your favours to me, favours of which I have had experience in the past."

Unfortunately the correspondent's reply has not survived, though the perplexities of a local practitioner in the pre-

Pasteur era when confronted with a malady as hideous as rabies are not difficult to imagine.

The incident described was by no means unique as further examples collected by Gaziot prove. During the revolutionary era many people were bitten by wolves in the neighbourhood of Nice, including a shepherd called Guiglion. The latter was treated by a physician, but failed to follow the prescription, and subsequently died as a result of the wound. Probably he would have died in any case as the doctor's remedies dated from the time of Dioscurides in the first century A.D. This wolf soon caused a reign of terror in the neighbourhood of Aspremont, and a little girl who was bitten likewise succumbed. The tragedy was mentioned in a letter from the mayor of Aspremont to the local prefect at the time. "A physician from Tourettes, Jules César-Massiera, was summoned to take care of the little girl, but he was too late, and the child, despite his efforts, died."

More recently a rabid wolf spread death and panic in Puy-de-Dôme. The winter of 1839 was of exceptional severity, and one December evening a doctor returning to the village of Fournols d'Auvergne through the wild mountain country of the Massif Central heard a wolf howling in the distance. He was familiar enough with the hideous sound as the beasts were relatively common in the district at that date, but on this occasion he felt his blood turn cold for he knew it was emitted by a mad wolf.

Next day a woman called Marie Margand was herding her cows near her home when an enormous wolf appeared and bit her savagely in the face. She was found by a man who spread the alarm just as a farmer arrived to announce that his herds had been attacked and he had only just succeeded in escaping with his life. The beast then savaged a stonemason who was also bitten in the face and died of rabies three weeks later. His final paroxysms were dreadful to see, and he was only narrowly prevented from attacking the priest who had been summoned to administer the last rites. The wolf's next victim was a forester, who was attacked while crossing a wood. He too died in frenzy, and by now panic had spread throughout the entire district.

The beast turned south and attacked a sawyer working near a pit. A terrible struggle ensued. The sawyer succeeded in trapping the wolf's head under his left arm, but failed to get a hand to his knife. When he begged the bystanders to give him a weapon they shrank away in terror and left him to his fate. Man and wolf finally tumbled into a well, and during the ensuing mêlée the animal escaped. At first the sawyer appeared to have got off lightly apart from a bite on his ear. But even the slightest scratch could prove fatal with rabies, and three weeks later his neighbours were shocked to see him running naked through the village. As he ran he warned everyone that he intended to drown himself and advised them to keep out of his way. He was finally arrested, but died in delirium a few days later at the early age of thirty-nine.

The wolf still wet from its immersion in the well next attacked a boy and three women. All four subsequently died. It then moved west towards Charraux and surprised another boy who was busy chopping wood. His cries for help were heard by an old widow-woman who immediately ran to his aid. After biting her in the cheek the wolf made off and attacked a man called Nigon. Seizing the beast in his arms this tough young peasant attempted to suffocate it by thrusting his arm down its throat. But the wolf broke free and made off towards Les Hayes, leaving its three latest victims to die like the others.

When it attacked a flock of sheep a shepherdess nursing her baby boldly attacked it with her fists. After mauling her severely the wolf picked up the infant, but fortunately abandoned it to attack the mother again. However, before it could close the woman seized the baby and managed to escape with it back to her cottage. Having ascertained to her almost incredulous joy that the infant had suffered no harm, she heated a pot of olive oil to boiling point and plunged her arms into the scalding fluid. The agony of the immersion almost made her faint, but the prompt cauterization saved her from rabies.

The wolf next bit a mother of eight children on the lip and hands, and she died of rabies as did three others. Continuing north it encountered two young sisters and after knocking them down it scratched them with its paws. One, however, chanced to be carrying a pitch-fork and eventually succeeded in driving the beast away. It then finally turned north-westward, returning like a hare to its point of departure. After savaging some cattle it attacked a party of women and children engaged in washing clothes, but mainly only their garments suffered and all of them escaped. These were the beast's last human victims, for later it disappeared. Then one day in January some hunters discovered a dead wolf lying in the forest. As the hounds declined to approach its remains it was generally supposed to be the rabid animal which had finally succumbed to its fatal malady.

Some forty years later a similar drama took place in the canton of Indre. At five o'clock on the morning of 17th July a rabid wolf attacked a woman called Joséphine André, who was severely bitten while attempting to protect her dog and sheep. Half an hour afterwards it bit a goat and a dog and attacked a second woman who was fortunately protected by her thick clothing. It then moved on to another village where it attacked a flock of sheep. At 6.30 it attacked several dogs and cows and a shepherd boy who hastily climbed a tree. Having a piece of bread in his pocket the boy threw it down to the raging animal in the hope that it would go away. In fact it soon flew off towards another village and, after maiming a flock of sheep, attacked a woman minding some cows. The unfortunate woman received serious wounds both in her arms and breast. At 9 a.m. some four hours after the original assault, it attacked a sow and bit a woman in the thigh. The woman's small son happened to be playing nearby and the wolf immediately knocked him over, but before it could harm him the sow ran up and charged its mortal enemy. The child escaped, but the sow was so badly bitten that it had to be destroyed.

The wolf next bit a girl in the shoulder, but before it could maul her some labourers arrived and put it to flight. At 10 a.m. it bit a dog, a lamb and a goat, and an hour or so later it wounded a heifer. It was next observed by a road-man who was searching for a shovel he had lost in a copse. But the beast left without attacking him, and ignored a party of harvesters working nearby. Clearly, though frenzied, it still possessed sufficient cunning to choose the weaker victims. At 2 p.m. it attacked a little girl of seven called Marguérite Gay. It mauled her chest and shattered her collar bone but her shrieks for help brought her mother on the scene. The frantic woman at once engaged the savage creature, which repaid her by removing part of her face and fracturing her nose. At 6 p.m. the wolf reached the Bois-Cadet. A man called Henri was working in an adjacent field when the cry "Wolf!" reached him, but before he could raise his sickle the beast had knocked him down. A grim struggle followed with wolf and peasant at death grips rolling over on the ground. For a time the doughty Henri managed to cling to his ferocious opponent, but the wolf struggled furiously and tore away his thumb. The man was then forced to abandon his hold, whereupon the beast bit off an ear, mauled his face and wounded him deep in the shoulder. Leaving its stricken victim it next attacked a herd of cattle all of which subsequently went mad.

At 7.30 that evening some farmers were taking their evening meal when they heard a noise outside. It was caused by a flock of terrified sheep seeking refuge in the farm-yard. Guessing that the animals were being pursued by a wolf, one of the company, a boy of seventeen called Foulatière, seized a pitch-fork and rushed outside. As the last sheep went by the youth lunged at the wolf and struck it in the neck. The unexpectedness of the assault knocked the beast over, but it soon regained its feet and returned to the assault. By prodding it with the fork the gallant Foulatière succeeded in keeping the wolf at bay until help arrived. A blow from a scythe opened its belly as it crouched against a hedge, but even with its intestines showing the beast continued to show fight. Then Foulatière's mother arrived with an axe which she handed to the scytheman who split its skull. Yet still the wolf refused to die, but continued to struggle, panting horribly, while the farmers' pitch-forks pierced it through and through. When it finally succumbed its corpse was left where it fell and covered with hawthorn to prevent the dogs nosing it out. Such was the end of the savage creature which had terrified a whole district for the space of a single day.

An official autopsy was performed on the wolf's remains. Like the Beast of the Gévaudan it too was of a reddish hue, and was a male of about four years old. It was extremely thin, a characteristic of rabid beasts, and stood three feet high at the withers. The unfortunate Henri's ear and thumb were duly found in its stomach, but the physician, Monsieur Fillay, refrained from revealing that the wolf was mad so as not to alarm the victims. But the fatal malady was not to be gainsaid, and Madame Gay after refusing all food died horribly bathed in saliva. Little Marguérite survived for six months longer, and then, like the brave Henri, also died.

Foulatière went on a tour of the neighbourhood carrying the wolf's head in a bag in order to receive rewards from the grateful inhabitants. He collected a sum of 150 francs, but could never produce the mask without emotion. When the story reached Paris the proprietor of the *Figaro* presented him with a diploma for bravery and a silver medal. Foulatière survived for many years, and was still alive in 1929.

But Indre was not the only district in France that suffered from rabid wolves. The beasts were plentiful in the province of Haute-Vienne during the eighteenth and nineteenth centuries, and frequently attacked human beings. One June day a blacksmith called Gévy was walking through a clump of chestnuts when he suddenly met a wolf. As luck would have it he was carrying a gun, but his shot only wounded the beast. It immediately charged him and savaged his face. Gévy fled for his life, but even as he ran the wolf's assaults continued. It pursued him right up to his cottage door when his wife hearing his cries ran to his aid and killed it with a pick. At the time no one realized that the animal was infected, but ten weeks later poor Gévy went mad. His convulsions were so terrible that he was imprisoned in his room for the last few days before he died.

Further records of mad wolves have been preserved in Charente where many tragedies occurred during the nineteenth century. One autumn a report was received that a rabid she-wolf had attacked many animals and people in the neighbourhood of Barbezieux. The terror inspired by the beast's activities was such that the local inhabitants decided to combine with the object of hunting it out and destroying it. Meanwhile two women were leaving their house when one of them felt something tugging at her skirts. Turning round in the darkness she was horrified to find a huge wolf in the act of attacking her. Her cries brought her husband to the door, who immediately closed with it and bore it to the earth. After a titanic struggle the man eventually succeeded in locking the wolf's muzzle between his knees. His shouts for help brought some neighbours to his aid armed with a pike and a roasting spit. A blow from the latter despatched the wolf which breathed its last with the brave husband still clutching it. He had been badly mauled and at the insistence of the local prefect a skilled doctor was summoned to treat his wounds. At the same time he was voted a reward proportionate to the services he had rendered the community by ridding the district of the dangerous beast. Whether he survived we are not told, though the wolf was undoubtedly rabid. Rabies spreads quickly, and during the same year another she-wolf bit several children near Cognac, and finally attacked a youth and a girl. The latter was horribly mutilated, for in addition to deep wounds in the neck and face, one of her hands had been virtually eaten. Later the wolf was killed by blows from an axe when it attacked a farmer.

Next a wolf emerged unexpectedly from a neighbouring forest and caused a reign of terror on the outskirts of Ruffec. After attacking and terribly mauling two women returning from market, it wounded two others near the village of Les Adjots. These events aroused the populace who pursued it in company with the local gendarmerie, and surprised it attacking some pigs and sheep. Two peasants armed with muskets then arrived on the scene, and although the piece of one misfired the other was able to shoot it. They received a reward of 80 francs each for their prompt action. The elder of the two women attacked at Les Adjots succumbed to her wounds.

Some years later a second wolf appeared in the region of Ruffec and bit four women. One survived the attack by only forty-eight hours, and two others by a few days. All displayed symptoms of rabies, and all were the mothers of families. As a result of these attacks an official request was made for a grant of money to support the children and also for the organization of battues by the lieutenant appointed to deal with the wolves.

Ten years passed by and then a rabid wolf was seen in the district of Corrèze by a peasant who hailed appropriately enough from a village known as Saint-Germain-le-Wolf. Although he was unarmed he at once engaged the beast and a mortal struggle ensued. Fortunately several farmers rushed to his assistance, and the wolf was driven away. It was killed some days later, but the poor peasant soon displayed symptoms of rabies, and so terrorized his wife and family of seven children that he was arrested by the gendarmes and finally put to death.

Near Dirac one June a rabid wolf attacked a donkey owned by a peasant woman. When she tried to drive it off with stones it promptly attacked her. She was eventually rescued by some neighbours, though not before she had been savagely bitten.

"If only I had had my reaping-hook," she lamented, "the wolf wouldn't have got off scot-free." A few days later she died of rabies.

At about the same time a rabid wolf attacked several people in the commune of Bouex. A woman was badly bitten, and a peasant who went to her rescue owed his life to a friend who arrived with a pitch-fork and managed to kill the beast.

One September during the middle of the last century a man called Renaud was returning to his village after attending the local fair when a huge wolf surprised him in a wood. It made off after mauling him, and he arrived at his cottage minus his cheek and nose. He was taken to hospital while a posse of gendarmes set out in pursuit of the attacker. In the meantime the rabid creature had attacked some peasants not far away. One of them seized the wolf in his arms, and his father, hearing his cries, arrived with a gun and several neighbours. The wolf was shot and killed, but the youth, who had been badly bitten, was admitted to hospital with what result we do not know.

Some years later a rabid wolf attacked a shepherdess guarding her sheep. Her screams attracted another girl who ran to her rescue waving a crook, and succeeded in driving the beast away, but not until it had bitten the shepherdess in the nose. Later it maimed some sheep in another herd but it was never hunted down or destroyed.

Near La Rochette in the late seventies a tragedy occurred of such horror that it gave the local children nightmares for upwards of a generation. A little girl of ten called Marie Favreau was sent by her parents one October morning to cut green maize near the forest of La Braconne. She was accompanied by a boy of similar age called Firmin Fontroubade whose task was to gather acorns for his father's pigs. The pair noticed a small oak covered with acorns, so Firmin climbed up and shook the branches while the little girl collected the nuts below. Suddenly an enormous wolf appeared, so tall that it brushed the boy's dangling feet. Leaping at Marie it knocked her down before seizing her head in its jaws. It began to eat her. The boy in panic clung fast to the trunk screaming "Wolf!" at the top of his lungs in the hope that someone would come to the rescue. A peasant called Texier heard his cries, and ran, though he was unarmed, to the boy's assistance. The wolf was busy tearing little Marie to pieces when Texier arrived, but it at once attacked the newcomer. The boy then witnessed a terrible struggle. Though Texier was only a little man he made up in determination for what he lacked in strength. Aiming a kick at the wolf which threw it off balance he courageously leaped astride the snarling body and hugged it closely to him. When the beast seized his arm he attempted to stifle it by forcing the torn limb down its gullet. With his free hand meantime he belaboured the wolf with blows from his heavy sabot. But this treatment merely resulted in increasing its fury, and soon the brave peasant must have forfeited his life. Fortunately the boy's cousin had also been alerted by his cries, and although he was only armed with a stick he immediately went to the other's assistance. When the boy saw his cousin he dropped down from the tree and together they succeeded in stabbing the wolf to death. Texier by now was at the end of his tether and bleeding from more than fifty cuts, whereas the rescuer sustained only an injured finger.

An autopsy was performed on the wolf's remains, and it turned out to be a female. Its stomach contained strips of the little girl's flesh which were still undigested. It was also revealed that it had previously savaged a herd of cows and torn some clothes which a farmer had dumped in a field.

Texier received a reward and proudly displayed the wolf's skin in the neighbouring villages where he was loaded with money and gifts. A doctor from Rochefoucauld had cauterized his wounds and as they quickly healed it was generally supposed that he had escaped the fell contagion. But a month after the struggle he suddenly displayed a strange aversion to water which is the characteristic first symptom of rabies. His ravings became so terrible that he was given a drug and suffocated between two feather-beds. He left behind two sorrowing parents and a young wife expecting a baby.

When the boy's cousin received news of Texier's fate he departed in alarm with his wife and child to visit a healer in Chamonix. True he had only suffered damage to a finger, but the virulence of rabies rendered even the smallest wound suspect and he was anxious to have it examined. But he was already too late, and collapsed and died within a few hours of his arrival.

It is impossible to render sufficient homage to the courage of these two men who deliberately sacrificed their lives in order to preserve others from a horrible death. Their descendants still live at La Rochette, and their wives remained faithful to their memory and never remarried, preferring to devote their lives to the children so cruelly orphaned in a grim but heroic cause. Many years later the celebrated French historian Madame Cadet, who recorded the incident, recalled the sombre vision of her great aunt Florine, the living image of grief and resignation, who was one of the widows.

*Chapter Eight*

# Wolf Howls in London

ONE day, before the First World War, a cabby parked his hansom by the kerb on a main London thoroughfare and went off to have a drink. The horse, which had been strangely restive ever since they had entered the neighbourhood, now broke out into a sweat and displayed all the symptoms of extreme terror. Suddenly without warning it broke away and careered like a mad thing down the road. It was halted with difficulty by a constable, but nothing would persuade it to return to its place. When its owner put in a belated appearance the bobby shook his head.

"Should have known better," he growled admonishingly, "than to park outside the Zoo."

"What's the matter with the Zoo then?" the cabby rejoined defensively. "'E can't see the hanimals from 'ere."

"No, but 'e can 'ear 'em," the policeman answered gravely, handing back the reins. "'Orses know when them wolves start 'owling. Jest listen to 'em now." As he spoke the eerie sound was borne on the breeze and several other horses trembled violently and tugged at their halters. A horse's reaction is quite uncontrollable when it hears or scents a primeval foe.

Men, of course, react in much the same way. On 22nd February 1961 great excitement was caused near Clapham Common when a tame wolf escaped from confinement. It was one of a pair kept by a lady in a wired-in enclosure at her home. The cry "Wolf!" had not been heard in London for more than a thousand years, yet an atavistic memory of a far-off age when the grey outlaws lurked in the forests of

Epping and Richmond still ruffled the subconscious of the citizen body. Children familiar with the awful fate of Red Ridinghood's grandmother fairly flocked to the common when the news got abroad, only to learn to their disappointment that the poor frightened animal had become trapped in in a gap between the walls of St. Paul's churchyard and an adjacent hostel. The police, fully alive to the danger if the wolf ran amuck among a crowd of excited children, closed the footpath to people passing through before boarding up the gap. Next they dragged heavy nets to the top of the churchyard wall to be dropped over the beast. Finally a constable wearing heavy gloves managed to slip a loop over the wolf's head. But the shock proved too much and the wretched creature died of heart failure as the police tried to lift it clear. For once it was possible to feel sorry for a wolf, though such occasions are infinitely rare.

A thousand years ago wolves were common in the great forests of central England, and during January, called "Wolf Month" by the Saxons, packs of hungry beasts roved the wild country north of the Thames. Indeed the menace was so great to travellers leaving the city that a special grant of land was made by the good Abbot Leofstan of St. Albans to one Thurnoth and others in return for keeping the woods between the Chiltern Hundreds and London free from wolves.

In some places where the presence of wolves constituted a special danger "hospitals" were set up for the protection of travellers. One of the most notable was built in the time of Athelstan in Yorkshire, and a farm at Flixton is called "Spittal" to this day. According to one authority, Blaine, records still existed at Flixton, Hackston and Folkston in the middle of the last century of payments made for the destruction of wolves at fixed rates per head. "They used," he says, "to breed in the 'cars' (fenny copses) below, amongst the rushes, furze and bogs, and in the night-time to come up from their dens, and unless the sheep had been previously driven into the town, or the shepherds were indefatigably vigilant, great numbers were sure to be destroyed." Indeed as late as the end of the fourteenth century Robert Umfraville held the castle of Herbotell and the manor of Otterburn in return for keeping the valley of Redesdale free from wolves. Also the rolls of Whitby Abbey of about the same time include an entry for payment for the tanning of fourteen wolf skins.

Battlefields were ever the happy hunting grounds of wolves, and tradition has it that the bodies of the English who fell at Hastings were devoured by the savage denizens of the Weald. The Normans, too, were destined to suffer a like fate when three thousand fell fighting against Waltheoff the Dane and provided a choice banquet for the wolves of Northumberland. Again, if we can believe Shakespeare or his sources, "loud howling wolves" greeted the Duke of Suffolk when he landed at night near Dover. Indeed, during the Middle Ages all the wilder parts of England appear to have been infested by wolves, including the Devonian peninsula.

In the latter connection it is interesting to note that when after the Second World War the army applied for additional training areas on Dartmoor, the local farmers were not slow to remind the authorities of the existence of a certain charter in Exeter cathedral. This had been issued under the seal of the future king John and gave them leave "to hunt the roe-deer, fox, wild cat, wolf, hare and marten outside his own forest." At the same time a certain William Berivere obtained leave to enclose lands in Devon with freedom to hunt the wolf. These were powerful concessions in the eleventh and twelfth centuries, and the descendants of the men who had rid Dartmoor of wolves were quick to draw attention to their ancient rights. Curiously enough the tradition that "wild beasts" were once found on the moor still lives on in the villages, and was repeated to the author by his grandmother, who was born at South Zeal.

It is hard to realize nowadays that the type of conditions described in the previous chapters once obtained throughout

England. But from the earliest times everyone's hand was against the wolves, and they were soon exterminated in settled areas. Rigorous measures were taken to combat the dangerous pests, at least from the time of Edgar. The Normans found it expedient to make grants of land on condition that it was kept clear of wolves, while compensation was made to those injured in wolf-hunts in the time of Henry I. Again, under Henry II the success of the royal hunters against the wolves in the New Forest was recognized by pecuniary awards.

Edgar's measures had been directed against the wolves which flourished on the Welsh borders, but wolves still roamed the forests of Herefordshire four hundred years later. In 1167 John Cumin, *custos* for the Bishop of Hereford, is recorded as having received the then considerable sum of ten shillings for capturing three wolves. Three years later Norman, keeper of the Veltrars (i.e. a pack of mongrel hounds), and a certain William Doggett received a similar sum for capturing two wolves in the forests of Irwell. John's son Henry III made grants of land to such as rid them of wolves. One of these was William Cantelupe, baron of Bergavenny (Abergavenny) on the Welsh border, while Henry of Angage held the manor of Piddlesey in Leicestershire in return for undertaking the capture of wolves. William de Limeres again held a carucate of land in the county of Southampton for hunting the wolf with the king's hounds.

Later still, in the time of the first Edward, Sir John d'Engayne held land in Northamptonshire by service of hunting wolves "for his pleasure", while John Giffard of Brampfield was empowered to destroy all wolves throughout the land. Clearly the beasts were still sufficiently troublesome to persuade the king of the necessity of taking measures against them in the country at large. That the thickly forested areas of the western midlands provided ready harbours for wolves is shown by a firman issued to a certain Peter Corbet on the 14th May 1281. It was written in Latin and read as follows. "The king to all his bailiffs, etc., greeting. Ye are to know that we have enjoined our beloved and trusted Peter Corbet to capture and destroy wolves, wherever they may be found in all the forests, parks and other places within our counties of Gloucester, Worcester, Hereford, Shropshire and Stafford, by every means that should appear efficacious, employing men, hounds and his own native cunning, and for that reason we command you that you assist him with the same end in view."

The Fens again provided good cover for wolves, as well as store of wild fowl to eat, and in 1286 a certain Richard Engaine held one hundred shillings' worth of land in Cambridgeshire by the serjeantry of taking wolves. As he was requested to perform this service daily the number of wolves operating in the region must have been very considerable.

During the following century payments for killing wolves were included in the accounts of Bolton Abbey, while in the reign of Edward II a compact was made between Sir John Mowbray and the Abbot of Selby whereby the latter renounced all his rights in the manor of Crowle and other places apart from his "free warren of goats, foxes, wolves, conies, etc."

So wild a region as the Peak District in Derby was particularly infested, and a family surnamed Wolfhunt held lands by service there. Wolves lingered in the neighbourhood for many years, and the killing of the last wolf in England was claimed by the village of Wormhill.

During the reign of Edward III, Conan, Duke of Brittany, gave grazing rights for cattle in the district round Richmond (Yorkshire) to the abbey of Fors in Wensleydale, but forbade the monks to employ mastiffs to drive wolves from their pastures. This seems a harsh injunction, though it was partially ameliorated by the gracious permission to take the flesh of beasts that had been killed by wolves.

Robin Hood's erstwhile haunt of Sherwood Forest was also a notorious habitat of wolves, and a certain Alan de Wulfhunte held land for the service of destroying them in the district. They were finally exterminated during the fifteenth century by Sir Robert Plumpton, though they still survived in the counties of Northamptonshire, Rutlandshire, Oxfordshire, Essex and Buckinghamshire, a record which bears witness to the wide dispersion of the beasts. The same counties are mentioned in the time of Henry IV when Sir Thomas de Aylesbury held the manor of Laxton by favour of taking wolves.

In the time of Edward IV a certain Juliana Barnes wrote a treatise on hunting, hawking, fishing and heraldry, and included the wolf among official game:

> Foure manner bestys of venery there are:
> The fyrste of theym is the harte, the seconde is the hare,
> The boore is one of tho: the wulfe and not one mo.

The season for hunting the wolf was from 2nd December until 25th March, but the universal fear and execration in which the beast was held soon nullified any seignorial attempts to enforce a close season. Indeed, traps were set during the fourteenth century to catch the fierce killers that threatened the deer in the Cheshire woods.

With the advent of firearms the wolf's days in England were numbered. As the country was separated from Europe no fresh packs could wander in from other lands to reinforce the dwindling stock, save occasionally across the borders from Scotland and Wales. The precise date of its extinction is not recorded though it seems to have disappeared during the reign of Henry VII. Such at any rate is the verdict of *The Italian Relation*, a very interesting account of England as seen through the eyes of a foreign observer, published in that reign. "They have no wolves, because they would immediately be hunted down by the people: it is said, however, that they still exist in Scotland, as well as the forests of Caledon at the extremity of the island, towards the north."

Nevertheless Ambrose Barnes of Hatfield near Barnard Castle earned the nickname of "Roast Wolf" in Henry's time, from the numbers of beasts he had hunted down. Doubtless the wolves had received a reprieve during the Wars of the Roses when all organized hunting ceased, and only the active measures of such as Ambrose prevented the wolf menace from spreading afresh. The last were said to have been killed, as has been observed, in the Peak District, or amid the dark thickets of Macclesfield forest.*

Place names are apt to prove fallacious, but still many bear witness to the former existence of the wolf. Wolfscrag near Pulborough in Sussex is said to have been the scene of the slaying of the last wolf in the Weald, while three fields nearby are named significantly Great Den, Little Den and Far Den. There is a Wolfstones in Lancashire, a Wolferlow in Herefordshire, Wolfscotes in Derbyshire and Oxfordshire, and a Wolfhamcote in Warwickshire, but Wolverhampton despite the fame of its football club is disappointingly unconnected with wolves. The Bleeding Wolf Inn may commemorate the demise of a wolf in Cheshire, though inn names often represent popular corruptions of less familiar words.

Strange though it may seem, only one tragic story connected with wolves has survived in legend. One day—the date is not specified—the lord of Beckermont went wolf hunting in Cumberland accompanied by his lady. At some stage the pair became separated and as evening drew on the husband became anxious. A search was instituted but not in time to save the lady from the wolves. Though the tale is unique it doubtless commemorates many a forgotten tragedy connected with wolves in England.

* According to Mr. Ralph Whitlock (*The Field*, 5th December 1963) a "last wolf" was killed in the royal forest of Clarendon, near Salisbury, in 1328. But wolves survived in the north much later, and Whitaker mentions the forests of Blackburnshire and Bowland as among their last retreats.

*Chapter Nine*

# Welsh Wolf Mysteries

MUCH of Wales is wild even today. In medieval times it was naturally far more so, and in the great primeval forests of Brecon, Radnor, Merioneth and Snowdonia, as well as in Carmarthen and Pembroke, wolves still lingered. That they were normally neither common nor aggressive may be inferred from the account of Giraldus Cambrensis who traversed the country during the reign of John, and makes no mention of wolves. Indeed, references to wolves in Wales are tantalizingly few, though one can never be certain that fresh evidence bearing on their former existence may not turn up in some novel and exciting form.

In 1928 one of the most extraordinary survivals connected with wolves was mentioned in a letter to *The Field*. It consisted of two shrivelled pads, together with a wild boar's skull and the horns and hooves of a roebuck, which had been preserved in the chimney of the great hall of the Island House at Laugharne in Carmarthenshire from time immemorial. Nothing of their history was recorded, except that they had always been regarded as sporting trophies. About 1880 the then owner of the house had presented them to the local vicar, who had in turn passed them on to his successor. From the latter they came into the possession of a Mr. Congeve of Buxton, who, realizing their importance, sent them for examination to Mr. R. I. Pocock. This eminent zoologist, while admitting that there was no infallible method of distinguishing between the pads of a wolf and those of a large dog, was still doubtful whether anyone would have bothered to preserve the latter even had they belonged to a favourite hound. In fact, the practice of preserving wolf pads was well known in France, and the door of a building on the estate of the Comte de Montbron at Chaufailles in Corrèze is still covered, according to Monsieur Vincent, with the pads of wolves destroyed in hunting.

Assuming then that the pads were relics of a wolf killed in the neighbourhood the probable date of its death raises exciting possibilities. The roebuck survived in Wales until the sixteenth century and was not reintroduced for three hundred years, and although the date of the wild boar's disappearance cannot be accurately determined specimens still survived in the Chartley forest in Staffordshire in 1593, and in Windsor Great Park as late as 1617. There is, however, no valid record of wolves in Wales at such a recent date, though it is reasonable to suppose that they continued to exist in the wilder areas long after their extermination in England. The pads, incidentally, have since disappeared from the Carmarthen Museum where they were formerly deposited.

Curiously enough it was in the town of Carmarthen that a rabid wolf once bit twenty-two people, most of whom subsequently died. This event occurred, according to the *Annales Cambrenses*, in 1166, just a hundred years after the Battle of Hastings. After the examples already quoted from France and Russia it is surprising to learn that any of the victims survived. But that a wolf should have wandered into the town itself is in accordance with the known character of rabid specimens which abandon all their fears of man, and boldly invade their dwellings. The attack of 1166 was recorded presumably because the victims were so many, and because the assaults took place in a crowded town. But that such attacks occurred elsewhere in remoter villages with less spectacular results is scarcely to be doubted.

Carmarthen again was associated with a monument that formerly existed near the town. An old photograph showed a stone erection of considerable size near the spot where the last Welsh wolf was killed. Sir Hugh Rankin referred to it recently in a letter to *The Field*, in which he stated that the wolf in question was killed in the reign of Henry VIII. Unfortunately the monument has since disappeared, and faded from local memory. This could have been the beast whose pads were preserved at Laugharne, as the house is supposed to date from 1500 or a little before. Much of course depends on the authenticity of the rubric on the monument, as well as that of the monument itself, but there seems no reason to doubt that wolves may have survived in Wales down to this period, and possibly even later.

Officially wolves were largely exterminated in Wales during the reign of Edgar in the ninth century.

> He, Edgar, imposed a tribute upon the King of Wales, exacting 300 wolves. This tribute continued to be paid for three years, but ceased upon the fourth, because he stated that no more could be found.

So wrote William of Malmesbury. Holinshed's version is as follows:

> The happie and fortunate want of these beasts in England is universallie ascribed to the politike government of King Edgar, who to the interest the whole countrie might once be cleansed and clearelie rid of them, charged the conquered Welshmen (who were then pestered with these ravenous creatures above measure) to paie him a yearlie tribute of woolfes skinnes, to be gathered within the land. He apportioned them thereto a certaine number of 300, with free libertie for their prince to hunt and pursue them over all quarters of the realme; as our chronicles doo report. Some there be which write Ludwall, Prince of Wales, paid yearlie to King Edward this tribute of 300 woolfes, whose carcases being brought into Lloegres, were burned at Wolfpit, in Cambridgeshire, and that by meanes thereof within the compasse and terme of foure yeares, none of these noisome creatures were left to be heard of within Wales and England. Since this time, also, we read not that anie woolfe hath beene seene here that hath beene bred within the bounds and limits of our countrie: howbeit there have been diverse brought over from beyond the seas for greedinesse of gaine, and to make monie onlie by the gasing and gaping of our

people upon them, who covet oft to see them, being strange beasts in their eies, and sildome knowne (as I have said) in England.

Powel refers more succinctly to the same event:

> In the year 965 the country of North Wales was cruelly wasted by the army of Edgar, King of England; the occasion of which was the non-payment of the tribute that the king of Aberffraw, by the laws of Hywel Dda, was obliged to pay to the king of London. But at length a peace was concluded upon these conditions, that the king of North Wales, instead of money, should pay to the king of England the tribute of 300 wolves yearly; which creature was then very pernicious and destructive to England and Wales. This tribute being duly performed for two years, the third year there were none to be found in any part of the island, so that afterwards the prince of North Wales became exempt from paying any acknowledgement to the king of England.

The statement that wolves were thereby exterminated throughout the length and breadth of the kingdom is manifestly absurd, seeing that the beasts survived in Scotland and Ireland into the eighteenth century, and in England until the time of Henry VII. Even in Wales itself they were not so easily got rid of as the evidence from Carmarthen and elsewhere proves.

The scene of the legend of Prince Llewellyn and his faithful hound Gelert is set in Snowdonia at the village of Beddgelert. The story exists in several versions, but one of the best known is given by Borrow.

> Llywelyn during his contests with the English had escaped with a few followers to the valley, and one day departed with his men on an expedition, leaving his infant son in a cradle in his tent, under the care of his hound Gelert, after giving the child its fill of goat's milk. Whilst he was absent, a wolf from the mountain, in quest of prey, found its way into the tent, and was about to devour the child, when the watchful dog interfered, and after a desperate conflict, in which the tent was torn down, succeeded in destroying the monster. Llywelyn returning at evening found the tent on the

ground and the dog, covered with blood, sitting beside it. Imagining that the blood with which Gelert was besmeared was that of his own son devoured by the animal to whose care he had confided him, Llywelyn in a paroxysm of natural indignation, forthwith transfixed the faithful creature with his spear. Scarcely, however, had he done so when his ears were startled by the cry of a child from beneath the fallen tent, and hastily removing the canvas he found the child in its cradle, quite uninjured, and the body of an enormous wolf frightfully torn and mangled lying near. His breast was now filled with conflicting emotions, joy for the preservation of his son, and grief for the fate of his dog, to whom he forthwith hastened. The poor animal was not quite dead, but presently expired in the act of licking his master's hand. Llywelyn mourned over him as over a brother, buried him with funeral honours in the valley, and erected a tomb over him as over a hero. From that time the valley was called Bethgelert.

The event here described is usually said to have taken place in the time of King John, but as similar legends are found elsewhere in the world doubt has been cast on its authenticity. Baring-Gould recounts a Sanskrit story in which a woman charged her husband to keep an eye on the baby while she went out. But the husband went off begging. When the woman returned she was horrified to be greeted by the tame ichneumon (a small carnivorous mammal resembling a weasel) with its mouth dripping with blood. She slew it with a blow from a pail, only to discover too late that the ichneumon had been responsible for saving the baby's life by engaging and destroying a dangerous snake. When the story reached Europe a dog was substituted for the ichneumon, and the snake became a wolf. Gelert's grave is likewise under suspicion, as there is good reason to believe that it was erected by an enterprising landlord of the adjacent Goat Hotel! But when due weight is given to the element of *Märchen* it is still difficult to resist the conclusion that some notable episode involving a wolf gave rise to the local legend.

Apart from the story of Gelert the evidence for wolves in

North Wales is surprisingly scanty. According to Giraldus, a contemporary of Llywelyn, a Welshman was slain on the borders while attempting to pass through Henry II's invading army. His faithful greyhound refused to forsake his corpse, but stoutly defended it from the attacks of dogs, wolves and birds of prey. The English were so impressed by this show of faith that they granted the Welshman honourable burial.

Again, according to Pennant, a ditch near Abergele was called Ffoi y Bleiddiaid—Wolves' Ditch—probably from the frequent occurrence of the beast in those regions. But Welsh place-names are even more deceptive than their English counterparts, as Blaidd was an ancient personal name as well as the Welsh for wolf. But there can be little doubt about Cil y Blaidd—Wolf's Lair—or Pant y Blaidd—Wolf's Hollow—on the Pembrokshire-Carmarthenshire border, Camfa'r Bleiddiau—Wolf's Leap—on the Irfon, and Wen Bleiddiau—Wolves' Glen—in Breconshire. Nant y Fleiddiast —Brook of the She-Wolf—is a tributary of the Towy, while there is a Wolves' Glade in Montgomeryshire, a Wolf's Stronghold in Carmarthenshire, and a Wolf's Rill and Wolf's Pit in Pembrokshire. The last wolf in South Wales was killed at Reynoldston in the Gower peninsula or at Pant y Blaidd near Marros mentioned above. Other "last wolves" were recorded at Cregina in Radnorshire and at Tyla-coch mountain near Treorchy.

Of Cregina the Rev. D. Edmondes Owen writes:

> When Henry III held his Court in the great castle of Matilda de Braose on one of the heights of Elwel he issued a royal command that his subjects in those parts should bestir themselves to destroy the wolves which were far more numerous and destructive there than in any other part of the realm. The wolf, even at that distant date, was beginning to fall back upon those hospitable and settled regions for sanctuary. There he continued to wage an uneven war against the sturdy and agile hillsmen, right down to a late date in the Tudor period when, according to a marginal note in one of the lost registers of Cregina, the last wolf in the county was killed on one of the steep hills overlooking the Edw.

Yet despite the beast's official extinction traditions of its local survival in Wales lingered on right down to the eighteenth century. According to George Owen, writing in 1603, "the wolfes are banished the lande." But such negative generalizations must be treated with caution. Mr. Sydney Moore states that when he returned to the Massif Central in France in 1933 he saw a wolf though the beasts were popularly supposed to have been long extinct in the area. Indeed, when he made inquiries in the local villages the peasants stolidly maintained that none existed.

An extraordinary story was rife in Merioneth. In his book on the county, *Cantref Meirionydd*, Robert Prys Morris gives the following account of the killing of a wolf in the parish of Dolgelley at a place known as Ogo'r Fleiddiast—The She-wolf's Den.

> The place which is named Twll y Fleiddiast is near or under an old tumbled down wall, separating the mountain of Cefn y ywen isaf and Cefn yr ywen ucha. Tradition has it, a tradition that is almost dead, that a she-wolf and her cubs were killed in Ogo'r Fleiddiast somewhere in the neighbourhood, and it is very likely that this is the spot referred to. It was about the year 1785. Many lambs were killed in the district, and because of this the son of Cefn yr ywen fawr, who lived near Cefn y ywen isaf and was regarded as a very good shepherd went with his brother to investigate the cause of the killing. The brother incidentally suffered from a speech defect. After seeing evidence of the killing the shepherd soon entered the cave to investigate, and warned his brother not to allow anyone to follow him. Having entered the cave he discovered the cubs, and began to destroy them. The howls of the cubs drew their mother's attention, but as she was rushing into the cave the guard caught hold of her tail. When the other brother heard the commotion he inquired what was the matter. His brother stammered that if he were to let go of the tail he would soon find out. Realizing his peril the shepherd at once attacked the beast and killed it.
>
> It was generally believed that wolves had become extinct in the mountains of Merioneth long before this. Nevertheless

my informant, who had investigated the tradition, was unable to date it otherwise. It is strange, however, that the event had been almost forgotten in the neighbourhood, unless of couse, as seems possible, it took place some years earlier. Camden, whose history appeared at the beginning of the seventeenth century, states that sheep grazed on the mountains of Merioneth without danger from wild beasts. It was thought that wolves had been destroyed when King Edgar levied a tribute of 300 wolf skins on the Prince of Gwynedd. This tribute was paid for two or three years—Camden states three on the authority of William of Malmesbury—but was stopped in the fourth owing to the lack of skins. In any case some remained according to reliable accounts. In fact the *Welsh Dictionary Encyclopaedia* under the word "Wolf," states that Edward I appointed Peter Corbet to destroy them. Edgar died in the year 975 and Edward in 1307.

What are we to make of this story? Leading authorities dismiss it altogether as a Welsh fabrication based on a tale already familiar in Scotland. But it is hard to see how the tale could have reached Wales, or become associated with such a remote region as Merioneth. Also the detail about the stammering brother is unique. Like circumstances of course tend to produce like events, and as both legends are concerned with wolves' dens the methods employed could have been similar in both cases. The date proposed, nevertheless, is quite past believing. That the wolf should have lingered in Wales in remote areas into the sixteenth century seems possible, but hardly into the seventeenth or eighteenth. It is true that it survived in Scotland and Ireland until the 1700s, but the above account is unique for Wales. At the same time, as with Gelert, one cannot help feeling that the story is founded upon some historical episode. The spot known as Wolf's Den may well have gained its name in some such circumstances, but probably a couple of hundred years earlier than 1785. The grey beast's tenacity and powers of survival over long periods are well authenticated, but the presence of a she-wolf with cubs presupposes a mate, and it seems quite incredible that the nucleus of a wolf-pack could have existed in the Principality for a considerable period without being detected.

It is strange that more legends have not survived either in Wales or England. But in a peasant society the presence of wolves, as in present-day Spain and Italy, is accepted as one of the hazards of nature, and excites as little interest as that of martens or foxes. It is only in hard weather when they descend from their fastnesses and attack sheep and humans that there is an outcry against them and they figure in the Press. In medieval times, when wolves were common, incidents connected with their hunting or destruction were clearly not regarded as of special account, and only tragedies of signal horror like the raid by the rabid beast on Carmarthen were deemed of sufficient importance to be recorded in the chronicles.

Apart from more active measures the destruction of the great forests that once clothed Wales uncovered the wolves' last retreats, for the *blaidd* was essentially a woodland creature, which only took to the hills as a last resort. This preference is clear from their habits in France, for it is interesting to note that they were relatively more common in the lowland forests of Indre, Vienne and Charente than in the higher districts of the Massif Central or the Haut-Pyrénees. Though the forests were not cleared primarily to expose the thickets which harboured wolves, as they were in Scotland in the sixteenth century, their removal in the interests of agriculture or ship-building were none the less conducive to the extinction of their feared and more noisome inmates.

Changes in climate too may have had some effect, for the wolf is in the main a cold climate animal, and the near arctic winters of the medieval period were not only more suited to its survival, but must have rendered its capture and trapping during the months when its attacks were most frequent and dangerous virtually impossible.

*Chapter Ten*

# Killer Wolves in Scotland

EAST of Aviemore rise the Cairngorm mountains, nowadays as famed for their ski-runs as for their rugged beauty. But the grim massif to the westward is ignored by winter sportsmen and mountaineers alike, for the peaks are not famous, and few roads or tracks pierce the gaunt fastnesses of the Monadhliaths. Thirty miles away lies the Caledonian Canal, but the wilderness between is innocent of croft or habitation, and of all creatures save eagles and deer. Among the lowering summits rises the Findhorn, one of the remotest and least known of highland streams. The name is Nordic, and of Norse-like proportions were some of the clansmen who roamed its banks and barren braes.

The hunter McQueen of Pall-a' Chrocain in the pass of Eanach, was reputed to have been "nearer seven than six feet high, proportionately built, and active as a roebuck." If there were daring feats to be performed, hazardous journeys to be undertaken, or beasts to be followed through the trackless glens, McQueen was sure to be summoned by the members of the Macintosh clan.

Then one winter's day in 1743 a poor woman, accompanied by her two children chanced to be crossing the hills from Calder. As they reached the wildest part of the pass a gaunt black shape suddenly emerged from a thicket behind a rock and leaped upon the children with a savage growl. Before their mother could come to their defence it had killed them both, but she managed to save her own life by running down the glen. Some hours later she stumbled into a cottage in Moyhall and poured out her tragic story.

At first no one could believe it. A wolf in the glen? Impossible. It was more than a generation since a wolf had been seen in the Monadhliaths, and it was commonly believed that the beasts had ceased to exist elsewhere. Yet there was the undoubted fact of the killing of the children which could not be otherwise explained. In the meantime the chief of the clan was informed, for if the creature in question was indeed a wolf other women and children were likely to be in danger.

Macintosh was fairly beside himself with rage and chagrin when the news reached him. That such a crime could be committed in the parish of Moy within his borders was an insult to the clan. The wolf must be hunted down and destroyed before other victims perished. He immediately despatched orders to all his clansmen and vassals to assemble at midday the next day above Fi-Giuthas, and organize a *tainchel* or gathering to drive the surrounding countryside. Next day the chiefs and clansmen assembled at the tryst, but to Macintosh's amazement and annoyance McQueen alone failed to put in an appearance. As he was usually foremost in any enterprise demanding courage or endurance his absence on this particular occasion was all the more unaccountable. That he had deliberately absented himself from such an exciting adventure as a wolf-hunt was unthinkable, yet his experience and dogs were considered so vital to the success of the enterprise that the assembly waited for him in mounting impatience until the better part of the day had gone. The scene is not hard to picture. The dark eager faces of the assembled clansmen, their dirks and claymores flashing in the sunlight, their chief chafing in the centre, irate and terrible in hunting tartan, his eagle eyes brooding on the distant hills. Suddenly the tall shadow of the missing carnach fell across the sward.

"Where have you been, ye laggard?" the chief demanded furiously in Gaelic. "Have ye no heard there's a wolf in the glen?"

"*Ciod e a' chabhag?* (What is the hurry?)" the giant inquired serenely, as though the presence of a savage beast were a matter which brooked delay. His reply roused the clansmen to angry retort.

"A wolf, a black wolf," they shouted. "Dinna-ye ken, mon? A wolf has killed two children above Calder."

"I am little used to wait thus for any man," the chief broke in, "and still less for thee, Pall-a' Chrocain, especially when such game is afoot as were are bound after!"

"What sort o' game are ye after, Macintosh?" the hunter pursued with maddening imperturbability.

"Why—the wolf," the chief answered, wondering whether McQueen could be deranged in his wits. "Didn't my messenger instruct you?"

"Och, aye, that's true," Pall-a' Chrocain replied with a good-humoured smile. "Troth I'd forgotten. But an' that be a'," he continued, groping among the ample folds of his plaid, "there it is for thee."

To the clansmen's astonishment he casually produced the wolf's black head, still warm and dripping. Mingled exclamations of astonishment and admiration burst from the assembled Highlanders as he displayed the bloody trophy before tossing it on the grass. He then described how he had at once informed himself of the place where the children had been killed, examined the wolf's tracks and formed conjectures about its haunt.

"As I came through the sloch (ravine) there," he continued as calmly as if he were describing some everyday occurrence, "I foregathered wi' the beast. My long dog there turned him. I buckled wi' him, and dirkit him, and syne whuttled his craig (cut his throat), and brought awa' his countenance, for fear he might come alive again, for they are very precarious creatures."

"My noble Pall-a' Chrocain," the chief cried in delight, "the deed was worthy of thee! In memorial of thy hardihood I here bestow upon thee Seannachan (a plot of land so called), to yield meal for thy good greyhound in all time coming."

That this solitary instance of a wolf's appearance should have occurred more than forty years after any other record of wolves in Scotland has led some authorities to cast doubt on the story's authenticity. But the evidence in its favour is strong. To begin with the very remoteness and extent of the Monadhliaths, covering as they do an area of 500 square miles, was an admirable place for a last hide-out, though the survival of a single beast inevitably presupposes the existence of others. Wolves, on the other hand, are known to travel great distances, and it is possible that McQueen's wolf had moved to the Monadhliaths from some other area. Lone wolves again are notoriously savage, and this one could have been rabid too though McQueen, at any rate, suffered no ill effects. The beast is described as "black" by Sir Thomas Dick Lauder, but the Gaelic word *dubh* can mean simply "dark-hued," as Colonel J. A. McQueen observed in a letter to *The Field*. Thus it would be an appropriate enough term to apply to a wolf, though no description survives of the colour of the British species. Probably like that of wolves elsewhere it was extremely variable. According to Colonel McQueen the arms of the McQueens of Corryborough, the residence of the clan chief which was situated only a few miles from the supposed site of the hunter's exploit, bears three wolf heads. This may of course be fortuitous, but the likelihood is that the slaying of the wolf was commemorated in this way. The Colonel met in 1951 the late Alexander McQueen on his croft on the Findhorn who said that his grandfather vouched for the truth of the legend. Dugald Macintyre, the famous authority on highland wild-life, stated in *The Field* that the story was first told to his father by his grandfather Alan who was born in 1745, only two years after the supposed date of the event. McQueen himself survived until near the end of the eighteenth century.

As wolves tended to occur in outlying districts where the inhabitants were for the most part illiterate, and the appearance of wild beasts, of whatever description, little out of the common, memories of their slaying either swiftly faded or survived in the coloured versions of popular tales. Whether McQueen's wolf was the last killed in Scotland is open to question, as Lord Morton, then President of the Royal Society, solemnly assured the famous naturalist Buffon that wolves still existed in the Highlands in 1756.

The last wolf to have been killed officially in Scotland was the one hunted in the wilds of Lochaber by Cameron of Lochiel in 1680. Cameron was the famous chieftain knighted by Charles II for his efforts in the royalist cause. He was a notable wolf-hunter, and it was largely through his efforts that the beast was finally exterminated. He is said to have killed the wolf with his own hands, which probably means that it was first brought to bay by his hounds, and then despatched with a dirk thrust delivered with all the strength and skill of the experienced practitioner. Though later records of wolves exist this event was evidently considered of sufficient importance to warrant the preservation of the animal in question. Nearly 140 years after the exploit its stuffed remains were still on view at the old London Museum. When the collection was dispersed and sold the catalogue of the contents included the following entry: "Lot 832. Wolf—a noble animal in a large glass case. The last wolf killed in Scotland, by Sir 'C' (E) Cameron." This unique trophy apparently excited no particular interest in 1818 (possibly it was believed that wolves still existed in the Highlands!) and when an inquiry was set on foot some forty years later no information respecting its whereabouts was forthcoming. That such a highly interesting object should have been discarded or destroyed seems highly unlikely, and the faint possibility that it still survives in some obscure corner of a country museum or manor house cannot be ruled out. But by now 284 years have passed, and it is doubtful whether any preserved specimen could survive for so long. It is of course to be infinitely regretted that no record of the beast's size or colour was made at the time. How it came to the London Museum in the first place is a mystery. One might have expected it to remain in Scotland, and in the proud possession of the Cameron family, unless the knight decided to present it to the king.

Though virtually extinct by 1680, at the beginning of the seventeenth century the wolf was still common enough in the wilder districts of Scotland. It was hunted by James VI as it had been by his mother, Mary Queen of Scots; and John Taylor, the Water Poet, observed it at Braemar in 1618.

"It was the space of twelve days," he says, "before I saw either house, cornfield, or habitation of any creature, but deer, wild horses, wolves, and such like creatures, which made me doubt that I should never have seen a house again."

It was about this time, or possibly some years later, that a wolf was slain by the laird of Chisholm at the spot subsequently known as the *Gleann Chon-fhiadh*—Wolves' Glen. It appears that a she-wolf had made her den in a cave in the glen, and when her cubs arrived she became the terror of the neighbourhood. Not content with raiding the crofters' livestock, she attacked the weakly and killed several people. Finally matters became so bad that the laird and his brother determined to kill her. Why they had delayed so long is hard to understand, except that wolves were generally regarded as "chancy" beasts, under the protection of the "de'il", and dangerous to hunt since a bite could prove fatal. At any rate, the two men eventually set out for Strath Glan, and succeeded in tracking the wolf to her den. Finding that she was abroad, the laird seized the opportunity to crawl into the cave, and despatch the cubs with his dirk. But their feeble howling was heard by their mother, who immediately flew to their rescue.

The younger brother was standing on guard outside, but the wolf's swift arrival took him by surprise, and his spear thrust failed to find its mark. The laird's situation was now far from enviable, but he managed to thrust his fist, which was happily protected by a steel gauntlet, between his adversary's jaws. A terrible struggle then ensued, but in the end the chief succeeded in reaching his dirk and giving the wolf a mortal blow.

Somewhere about the turn of the century another she-wolf and her cubs were killed on the eastern coast of

Sutherland. It is perhaps significant that "last wolves" tended to be shes, for when the males became extinct in France the females were prone to mate with dogs and produce fierce hybrid *"loup-chiens."* This wolf was tracked to a rock gully by two shepherd boys from western Helmsdale, who reported the fact to the father of one of them, a man called Polson. The gully formed the bed of a burn in Glen Loth, and there Polson discovered a concealed cave. The entrance was too narrow to admit a full-grown man, but the boys having satisfied themselves that the wolf was not at home succeeded in squeezing through the aperture. The floor of the cave was littered with bones and debris, including feathers and egg-shells, though it was hard to see much in the semi-darkness.

A faint yowling directed the boys' attention to a dark corner where six cubs were lying. When they informed Polson of their find he advised them to lose no time in destroying them before the dam returned. Too late! The howls had reached the ears of the watchful wolf which dashed up to the entrance where Polson was standing. He grabbed for his gun, but it was unhappily out of reach, for he had left it propped against a rock while he helped the boys down. Fearing that they were doomed he hurled himself forward at the furious beast, and prevented her from slipping through the fissure by grimly hanging on to her long bushy tail. The boys were naturally unaware of their deadly peril and the life and death struggle taking place outside. Yet despite the she-wolf's frantic efforts Polson succeeded in twisting the tail round his left arm, and preventing her from escaping. Finding himself in total darkness Polson's son inquired what was blocking the light.

"You'll know soon enough," the father panted in reply, "if the root of the tail gives way."

Meantime the desperate shepherd managed to grasp his knife and stab the wolf in the flank. This was too much and the maddened creature turned on her tormentor. Polson, fully alive to the fate which awaited the boys if he himself was overpowered, now pushed against the wolf, trying to bash its head against the rock. At the same time he continued to stab her with his hunting knife until she finally expired.

The resemblance of this story to the one already related in connection with a supposed wolf incident in Wales has raised the justifiable suspicion that the latter is merely a rehash of the former and has no claim to authenticity. But, as has already been remarked, like circumstances are apt to produce like measures, and the Welsh story, apart from the admittedly impossible date, cannot be entirely dismissed.

A similar story is told of Clury Macpherson, chief of Clan-chatten. While out deer hunting he lighted on a wolf's den and decided to kill the cubs. Posting his servant to keep watch Clury crawled into the hole. Suddenly the guard observed a dark shape threading the rocks below, and realized that the old wolf was returning. He watched her advance in mounting panic. He was petrified. What should he do? Warning the laird could now do no good unless he could also prevent the beast from entering the den. That he could only achieve by closing with it in bodily combat as it attempted to rush by. The thought of such a deadly encounter was too much for his craven heart, and without even a shout to advise his master of his approaching doom he incontinently took to his heels.

The clansmen were filled with sorrow when the servant returned alone, but were perfectly prepared to accept his tale. He had, according to his own account, fought desperately to save his chief, but the wolf had proved too strong for them both and Clury had been killed. A party quickly assembled to brave the wolf and bring back the chief's remains, but just as it was starting on its melancholy errand Macpherson, pale and sorely wounded, staggered down the glen. After describing how he had finally killed the wolf he revealed how the cowardly servant had left him to his doom. A roar of anger burst from the angry clansmen at the conclusion of his speech, and seizing the cringing miscreant, they dirked him to death before his master's pitiless gaze.

During the sixteenth century vast forests clothed the Scottish glens and in them the wolves bred unmolested until they became a menace to the entire realm. Royal edicts were issued, as in previous eras, commanding the lairds to destroy the wolves in their several domains, and offering rewards to the clansmen for each dead beast. One issued in 1577 reads as follows. "Ilka baron within his barony in gangand (hunting) time of the year sall chase and seek the quhelpes of Wolves and gar slay them. And the baron sall give to the man that slays the Wolfe in his barony and brings the baron the head, twa shillings. And when the baron orders to hunt and chase the Wolfe, the tenants sall rise with the baron. And that the barons hunt in their baronies and chase the Wolfes four times a year, and als oft as once Wolfe ben seen wothin the barony. And that na man seek the Wolfe with schott, but allanely in the time of hunting them."

The clause stating that wolves should not be shot out of season seems curious in the circumstances, but shows that despite its depredations it was still regarded in the main as a legitimate quarry. The forests of Ross, Inverness, Cromarty, Perth, Argyll, Moray, Nairn, Lochaber and Rannoch were particularly infested with wolves, and it is recorded that as recently as 1848 old people recalled how their ancestors had regarded the forests on the Blackwater and Rannoch moor as virtually impassable through wolves. Indeed the howl of rutting wolves in the autumn must have been as familiar a sound to the local crofters as to the peasants of Charente in the nineteenth century. One of the most notorious haunts of wolves was the route across the mountains to Braemar via the Devil's Elbow. There a hospital was built for the protection of travellers, which still bears the name of the Spittal of Glenshee. Harrison, a historian of the Elizabethan period, laments that though the English "may safelie boast of their securitie in respect to wild animals, yet cannot the Scots do the like in everie point within their kingdome, sith they have greevous Wolves and cruell foxes, beside some other of like disposition continuallie conversant among them, to the general hindrance of their husbandmen and no small danger unto the inhabitants of those quarters."

William Barclay of Aberdeen, who spent his early years at the court of Mary Queen of Scots was present at a royal hunt in 1563, which was organized by the Duke of Atholl. An army of two thousand beaters was assembled to beat the forests of Atholl, Badernach, Mar and Moray, and when a wolf was unharboured the Queen herself ordered one of the fiercest hounds to be slipped at it. The hound in question would doubtless have been a Scottish deer-hound, a lighter version of the Irish wolf-dog, which could run down a wolf like a Borzoi.

Wolves were common in Strathnavern, according to Camden when he wrote of Scotland in 1586. "The country hath little cause to brag of its fertility. By reason of the sharpness of the air it is very thinly inhabited, and thereupon extremely infested with the fiercest of Wolves, which, to the great danger of the country, not only fiercely set upon cattle, but even upon the owners themselves, to the manifest danger of their lives. In so much that not only in this, but in many other parts of Scotland, the sheriffs and respective inhabitants are bound by Act of Parliament, in their several sheriffdoms, to go ahunting thrice every year to destroy the Wolves and their whelpe."

There was clearly only one recourse against the wolves and that was to burn or cut down the forests which harboured them. This was a mammoth undertaking, but the lairds and their clansmen did not relax their efforts until the last lurking places of the dreaded "wild dogs" had been exposed. Only then was the wolf doomed, and though it still held out in northern wildernesses of Sutherland and Caithness its days were clearly numbered. Harting records how a large pine forest was destroyed at the end of the sixteenth century on the south side of Ben Nevis. It extended from Lochaber to the Blackwater and the moor of Rannoch, and the effort required to clear it was of no light order. Clearly the local inhabitants were finally driven to take action by the intolerable presence of the ferocious wolves. Like measures were called for in the vicinity of Loch Sloi where a forest extending for twenty miles was deliberately razed to the ground.

By 1621 the reward for the destruction of the surviving wolves had risen to £6 13s. 4d., a considerable sum at the time, yet one which even so poor a kingdom was prepared to advance in order to rid the land of the last of the beasts. As late as 1661 wolf skins appeared in the Customs roll, when two ounces of silver was paid "for ilk two daker" (i.e. ten skins).

Remarkably few accounts of attacks on human beings have survived in Scotland. But then such outrages commonly occurred in the wilder districts among illiterate people. Nevertheless the constant danger of wolves to women and children was clearly as great as anywhere else, as Bishop Leslie of Ross recorded in 1570. "Our nychbour Inglande has nocht ane wolfe with quhilkes afore thay war mekk molested and invadet, bot we now nocht few, ye contrare, verie monie and maist cruel, cheiflie in our North cuntrey, quhair nocht only invade thay scheip, oxone, ye and horse, bot evin men, specialie women with barne, outragiouslie and fercelie thay ovirthrow." The best known instance is that of the unfortunate woman on the Findhorn, already recorded, and doubtless such tragedies were of frequent occurrence. Sometimes, however, it is pleasant to note that the wolf came off second best.

An old peasant woman of Cre-lebhan near Strui on the north side of Strath Glas was returning home one day near Christmas with a brand new girdle, the heavy iron plate used for baking in the north. She had stopped by a wood to gossip with some neighbours when she suddenly noticed a wolf's head peering hungrily out of a crevice. Before the beast could leap on its intended victim the woman with remarkable presence of mind struck it with the girdle. The blow was so hard that it brained the wolf, putting an end to its life.

Dugald Macintyre recalls a similar occurrence in Argyll.

An old woman was chopping wood when a wolf attacked her, and she killed it with her axe. The dates of neither event is recorded, though they possibly refer to the seventeenth century.

That wolves will frequently enter houses has been already noted in France. An extraordinary instance in Scotland was recorded by the ghillie Angus McDiarmid in *A Description of the Beauties of Edinarple and Lochearnhead* published in 1815. According to McDiarmid the oak forests were so extensive in olden times in the lowland country that they provided admirable cover for wolves, which would often raid the farms and cottages while the owners were working in the fields. One evening a labourer returning to his home was horrified on looking through the open window to see his child sitting on one side of the fire with a wolf on the other. The child was laughing and joking with the beast under the impression that it was some friendly dog.

Fearing that the wolf might leap at the child and tear him to pieces before his eyes the terrified father drew his bow and carefully levelled an arrow. Fortunately his aim was true, and presumably only the child was saddened by the unexpected end of its erstwhile companion.

As an instance of wolves' cunning McDiarmid also recorded the following tale. At about the same time as the previous story the herds of Glendochard were raided by cattle-thieves. One bull, however, managed to escape, and hid in a hovel some distance from the village. While seeking refuge there it was attacked by a wolf, but bravely engaged its savage assailant. Two men who happened to be passing observed the battle, and decided to rescue the bull. They went home to arm themselves with bows and arrows then returned and climbed up to the roof. The wolf had disappeared but it eventually put in an appearance, and they were staggered by its size which was double that of a normal beast. Then they realized that it was not one but two wolves walking in line "with a cross stick in their mouths." When they reached the bull they attacked in concert, but were at once despatched by a volley of arrows. Upon examining the carcases the men were amazed to discover that one of the wolves was blind. Clearly the original animal, having found the bull too big and strong to master, had solicited the assistance of its blind companion and guided it to the spot.

During severe winters wolves raided not only the living, but the dead. Indeed at Ederachillis on the coast of Sutherland the villagers were obliged to transfer their burial ground to a neighbouring island in order to prevent the beasts digging up the graves. This grim event was commemorated in a poem by Mrs. Ogilvy in *A Book of Highland Minstrelsy*.

On Ederachillis shore
The grey wolf lies in wait,
Woe to the broken door,
Woe to the loosened gate,
And the groping wretch whom sleety fogs
On the trackless moor belate.

The lean and hungry wolf,
With his fangs so sharp and white,
His starvelling body pinched
By the frost of a northern night,
And his pitiless eyes that scare the dark
With their green and threatening light.

He climeth the guarding dyke,
He leapeth the hurdle bars,
He steals the sheep from the pen,
And the fish from the boat-house spars;
And he digs the dead from out the sod,
And gnaws them under the stars.

Four wolves were killed in Sutherland between 1690 and 1700, one in the west on the lonely shores of Loch Assynt, the others at Halladale and in Glen Loth. A monument erected by the Duke of Portland on his estate near Berriedale in Caithness commemorates the killing of the Glen Loth wolf, as already described, and these were the last to be officially reported. The story of McQueen, however, suggests that odd wolves lingered on in the remoter regions for upwards of fifty years. Once the forests were gone the wolves were forced to take refuge in the mountain caves. There they were finally brought to bay, and disappeared from the list of Scottish fauna. Yet the wolf's extinction was still not yet complete in the British Isles, for it still survived in Ireland.

*Chapter Eleven*

# Wolf Packs in Ireland

*"tis like the howling of Irish wolves against the moon"*

AS YOU LIKE IT.

MR. JONATHAN GRUBB of Sudbury, who was born in 1807, described how his grandmother's uncle was once chased by wolves in Ireland much in the traditional Russian style. His name was Malone and he lived at Ballyraggin in County Kildare, not far from the lonely Wicklow Mountains. Wolves still ravaged the countryside in the early eighteenth century and attacked the farmers' stock when the winters were hard. One day in the winter of 1721 Malone rode off on business, only to be benighted on the way home. As he descended the hill some miles from the farm the eerie sound of a long-drawn howl reached him on the wind. The hand of fear closed on his heart as the awful sound drew nearer. Not only the peasants were starving, and already several women and children had been attacked by a pack of the hungry wolves which had done notorious execution among the stock of the outlying farms. Before all, as Malone well knew, wolves preferred horses, and if they were on the track of his steed, as he firmly suspected, he was in critical danger of his life. Scenting the wolves, the poor hunter broke out in a sweat, and galloped for home as if the devil were after it. A glance behind served only to confirm Malone's fears, as he glimpsed the pack's slant-eyes gleaming greenly through the dark. As it is virtually impossible to tire a wolf the rider's only hope lay in reaching home while the horse was still fresh enough to outpace its traditional enemy. Then he remembered the rise. Five good miles of level going lay between him and the farm, but it ended in a long steep slope, where the wolves would have the advantage. If the beasts caught him there when the horse was exhausted their joint doom was certain.

Frantically urging his steed to greater efforts Malone flew along like a Derby winner, but despite the hot pace the relentless pursuers still loped stolidly at the horse's heels. The maddened beast shied and whinnied with fright, while its master belaboured it like a demented jockey. Still a mile to go, and the pace was beginning to tell. As the horse bounded up the slope its speed was already noticeably slower, and suddenly to his horror the rider realized that the wolves were closing in from either flank. At any moment he expected to hear the horse shriek as a wolf's sharp teeth sank into its warm flesh. Just as he had abandoned hope the familiar shape of the farmstead loomed in the night sky. Yelling to his brother, "James, James! My horse is ate with the wolves!" Malone drove into the stable with the beasts snarling and leaping on the horse's hind-quarters. Quick as thought he dismounted and closed the doors, only to discover that in his haste he had also imprisoned several members of the pack. But he need not have worried. Wolves are cowards at heart, and never more so than when trapped or deprived of their liberty. In no time at all the erstwhile terrors of the night had abandoned their attacks on the horse, and were cringing and whining in a vain attempt to escape. Happily James Malone soon arrived upon the scene armed with a loaded gun, and the wolves were shot with the minimum of difficulty.

That such an exciting adventure could have occurred in Ireland less than two hundred and fifty years ago seems almost unbelievable. Yet according to a report published some years later in 1738 wolves still abounded too much in the country. Indeed the beasts were held in such terror by the local peasants that they actually prayed for their preservation in the hope that they might be willing in return to refrain from devouring them!

Despite all attempts to exterminate them wolves survived

well down into the eighteenth century, and an interesting account has been preserved in a biography published in 1829 of a contemporary method of hunting them. The author states that the wolves were so troublesome that the inhabitants were prepared to offer as high a reward for their destruction as for the capture of a notorious highwayman.

One Rory Carragh pursued alone and unaided the dangerous profession of wolf-hunter, which he preferred to practise at night. To assist him he employed strong half-bred greyhounds, the ancestors of the modern wolf-hounds, but leaner and less massive. The shepherds of Tyrone folded their sheep for safety in an area enclosed by a high stone wall, with gaps for entry and exit at either extremity. Strongly though the gaps were secured, wolves used to break in at night and slaughter the inmates until the farmers were at their wits end for a method to protect them. Finally they sent for Rory, offering him a sum greater than the usual reward if he succeeded in ridding them of what were generally believed to be the last two wolves remaining in the county of Tyrone. Rory accepted the task, and taking with him two wolf-dogs and a little boy, the only person he could persuade to assist him, he arrived at the fold just as darkness was falling.

"Now," said Rory, addressing the boy, "as the wolves usually attack the opposite extremities of the sheepfold at the same time I must leave you and one of the dogs to guard this one, while I go to the other. He steals with all the caution of a cat, and you will not hear him, but the dog will, and will positively give him the first fall. If you are not active when he is down to rivet his neck to the ground with this spear, he will rise up and kill both you and the dog."

That the cowardly farmers should have gone to their beds and allowed a small boy to face a wolf alone is only typical of eighteenth century manners. A boy was expendable, whereas farmers were not, and they doubtless retired without giving further thought to the matter. Today, of course, small children are left to guard flocks in Italy and Spain and no one thinks the worse of it. The boy, at any rate, was not deterred, and taking the heavy pike from the hunter's hand he gravely promised to do his best. Finally he opened the gate leading into the fold, and seated himself outside the entrance.

His hound crouched beside him on the alert, appearing to be perfectly aware of the dangerous mission upon which they were both engaged. The night was exceedingly dark and cold, and the poor little boy became so numbed by the chilly air that he was beginning to fall asleep. Suddenly with a roar the hound leaped across his prostrate form and launched itself at its mortal enemy. The boy was roused by the din, and the warning shout of his distant companion, and stabbed the wolf through its tawny neck before it could recover from its fall. As he did so Rory arrived waving the gory head of its mate. Such was the reputed end of the last wolves killed in County Tyrone, though the beasts continued to survive in the Wicklow Mountains, where the last was not killed until 1770.

Ireland is still a great hunting country, but in the early years of the eighteenth century the quarry was sometimes more exciting than the hare or the fox. A poem called "MacDermot," composed in 1719, describes wolf-hunting in Munster. The method used was clearly analogous to that formerly employed in India against wild boars.

> It happen'd on a day with horn and hounds
> A baron gallop'd through MacDermot's grounds,
> Well hors'd, pursuing o'er the dusky plain
> A Wolf that sought the neighbouring woods to gain:
> Mac hears th'alarm, and, with his oaken spear,
> Joins in the chase, and runs before the peer,
> Outstrips the huntsmen, dogs, and panting steeds
> And, struck by him, the falling savage bleeds.

Such a stirring account can hardly fail to rouse a faint sense of regret that a breeding nucleus of Irish wolves was not preserved in some remote area purely for hunting purposes. Unfortunately there is as little compromising with a wolf as with a hungry shark or eagle, and a rabid specimen, as we know from France, could soon decimate an entire county.

During the sixteenth century, as in Scotland, the wolf was extremely common in Ireland, a circumstance which, in the opinion of many, severely militated against proper government. For no one could be expected to farm or settle in a land where not only the herds and flocks, but the wives and children of the shepherds and farmers were constantly threatened. George Turbervile wrote in his *Booke of Hunting* published in 1575: "The Wolfe is a beaste sufficiently known in France and other countries where he is bred; but here in England they be not found in any place. In Ireland, as I have heard, there are great store of them, and because many noblemen and gentlemen have a desire to bring that countrie to be inhabited and civilly governed (and would God there were more of the same mind), therefore I have thought good to set down the nature and manner of hunting the Wolfe according to mine author."

Now the horse is as much the wolf's favourite prey as the zebra is the lion's, so the method usually adopted in Ireland was first to kill a horse as bait. The beast's forequarters were then lopped off and trailed through the woods to lay a good scent leading back to the carcase. Next day wolf-hounds were assembled in braces at the points where the wolves were most likely to appear, in order to prevent them regaining the safety of the coverts. When a wolf dashed out, following the scent, it was allowed to pass the first dog, which was then in a position to turn it if it attempted to break back, while the second was slipped "full in his face." Once the wolf began to run the remaining hounds were slipped in its direction so that "he was sure to be attacked on all sides at once, and therefore, the more easily taken."

Nevertheless such methods, though temporarily effective, were incapable of insuring the wolf's extermination, and in 1584 an order was issued at the instance of the Lord Deputy of Ireland, Sir John Perrott, in an endeavour to combat "the ravening and devouring wolves." It demanded that a clause should be inserted where a lease was granted requiring the tenant to "endeavour himself to spoil and kill wolves with traps, snares, or such devices as he may devise."

Despite these measures the wolf menace increased, and the flocks in Munster were devastated. Kilmalloch, a notorious haunt of wolves, was laid waste by James Fitzmaurice in 1591, but elsewhere the beasts throve. Fynes Moryson, Secretary to the Lord Deputy Mountjoy, records how at the turn of the century all cattle had to be stalled at night, for the wolves had become so daring that even the towns and villages were no longer safe. "The wolves are so much grown in numbers, as sometimes on winter nights they will come and prey in villages and the suburbs of cities."

During the reign of James I a bill was proposed for the destruction of wolves, but never actually became law. In 1619 matters were still as bad as they had been twenty years earlier and stock-owners were compelled to house their cattle at night "in the bawnes of their castles."

The situation, however, was not without its humorous side, at least, on rare occasions. Howell recorded in 1624 "a pleasant tale" related by Sir Thomas Fairfax concerning a soldier serving in Ireland. "As he past through a wood with his knapsack upon his back, being weary he sate down under a tree where he open'd his knapsack and fell to some victuals he had; but upon a sudden he was surpriz'd with two or three Woolfs, who, coming towards him, he threw them scraps of bread and cheese till all was done; then the Woolfs making a nearer approach unto him he knew not what shift to be at, but by taking a pair of bagpipes which he had, and as soon as he began to play upon them, the Woolfs ran all away as if they had been scar'd out of their wits. Whereupon the souldier said, 'A pox take you all. If I had known you had lov'd musick so well, you should have had it before dinner!'"

The wolf's unreasoning fear of music has, of course, been already noted in the case of the French fiddler who fell into the pit.

Between 1640 and 1650 wolves became so troublesome that even Cromwell could ignore them no longer. The magnificent Irish wolf-hounds had many admirers abroad, and it had become profitable for breeders to export them to England. The result was that the species had become rare in its own native country, a circumstance of which the wolves were naturally not slow to take advantage. So Cromwell issued a stern edict at Kilkenny in 1652 forbidding the export of the hounds.

> Forasmuch as we are credibly informed that Wolves doe much increase and destroy many cattle in several partes of this Dominion, and that some of the enemies party, who have laid down armes, and have liberty to go beyond sea and others, do attempt to carry away such great dogges as are commonly called Wolfe dogges, whereby the breed often which are useful for destroying of Wolves would (if not prevented) speedily decay. These are therefore to prohibit all persons whatsoever from exporting any of the said dogges out of this Dominion; and searchers and other officers of the Customs, in the several partes and creekes of this Dominion, are hereby strictly required to seize and make stopp of all such dogges, and deliver them either to the common huntsman, appointed for the precinct, where they are seized up, or to the governor of the said precinct.

A year later the dictator issued a second decree offering big rewards for the taking of wolves throughout Ireland.

> For the better destroying of Wolves, which of late years much increased in most parts of this nation, it is ordered that the Commandere in Chiefe and Commissioners of the Revenue in the several precincts doe consider of, use, and execute all good wayes and meanes how the wolves in the counties and places within the respective precincts may be taken and destroyed; and to employ such person or persons, and to appoint such daies and tymes for hunting the Wolfe, as they shall adjudge necessary. And it is further ordered that all such person or persons as shall take, kill, or destroy any Wolfes and shall bring forth the head of the Wolfe before the said commandere of the revenue, shall receive the sums

following—viz., for every bitch Wolfe, six pounds, for every dog Wolfe, five pounds; for every cubb which preyeth for himself, 40 shillings; for every suckling cubb, ten shillings. And no Wolfe after the last September until the 10th January be accounted a young Wolfe, and the Commissioners of the Revenue shall cause the same to be equallie assessed within their precincts.

The rewards were paid out of local taxes, a circumstance which caused hardship in districts where wolves were common. Indeed the inhabitants of Mayo petitioned the Council of State that the Commissioners of Assessment might be at liberty to come to some amicable arrangement about the settlement of rewards. These measures were evidently effective for henceforth the wolf became rare in Ireland, and by the end of the century was all but extinct. That hounds, despite the stringent regulations, were still being exported is clear from a letter written by Sir George Rawdon to Viscount Conway on the 11th July 1657, and quoted by Mr. W. H. Workman in the *Irish Naturalist's Journal*. After referring to other matters Rawdon mentions "the dogs which it is a pity to send out of the country especially one of them. They have been about 'The Collin' and above Mr. Doynes this six weeks, and had some courses at wolves which exceedingly infest this county."

A second letter dated 7th October 1665, from Lisburn refers to the wolves that roamed the shores of Lough Neagh. "The wolf haunts that park of late and hath killed 3 or 4 of a few muttons . . . so I have put Totnall upon setting traps and watching with guns and Simon the keeper who is an excellent shot but I perceive no great woodman, yet I hope will do well being careful and not given to drink.

"P.S. The keepers and all our gun men are watching the wolves that haunt the Tunny Park almost every night."

That the wolves had by no means disappeared is clear from the attempt made by Sir John Ponsonby in 1662 in a report to the Commissioners of Grievances to have a bill introduced in Parliament "to encourage the killing of wolves and foxes in Ireland." Seven years later the former were still described as "common," and in 1684 O'Flaherty included the wolf in the fauna of Connaught. During the reign of William and Mary, Ireland was still referred to as "Wolf-land," and a poem on the battle of La Hogue which took place in 1692 describes how:

> A chilly damp
> And Wolf-land howl runs through the rising camp.

Nevertheless the wolf's days were numbered, and "the last presentment [to the Grand Jury] for killing wolves" was made in 1710 in the county of Cork. Yet the complaint could still be made in 1738 that "wolves still abound too much," and their final extermination was delayed for a matter of fifty years or, some said, even later.*

Such is the history of the wolf in Britain as recorded by Harting and other competent authorities, and to naturalists it must read like a sad story. Wolves, however, and civilization do not go hand in hand.

* According to Mr. John Corbett (*Country Life*, June 6th, 1963) a wolf was killed in Co. Kerry in 1790, while another was killed in the Sperrin mountains as recently as 1810.

*Chapter Twelve*

# Grey Wolves of the North

STORIES about wolves in western Europe inevitably hold a romantic appeal, and must come as a salutary shock to such as were hitherto oblivious of the terror which formerly lurked at their door. But it would at the same time be absurd to pretend that wolves have not always constituted a far greater scourge in Russia, Poland and the Balkans, though details of their depredations have been harder to come by in recent years. The ordinary person associates Russia with wolves first and foremost, and is usually amazed to hear that they flourish at all elsewhere. The tradition is, of course, perfectly authentic, and wolves are almost as common in Russia today as they were in the time of the Czars.

A familiar tale describes how about the middle of last century the serfs driven to desperation by the oppression of the nobility finally decided to revolt. When the news reached the ears of a certain youth that his master and mistress were in mortal danger he was absolutely horrified, for the latter was young and beautiful and he had been kindly treated as a member of their household. At the same time it was more than his life was worth to reveal the secret which he had overheard, as all the other servants were in the plot, including the family butler. So it was with a sense of heavy foreboding that he mounted the carriage on which his employers were travelling to a distant estate. As they left the serfs formed up in line bowing deferentially, but with murder in their hearts. The party had scarcely arrived when it began to snow, and the servant felt thankful that they had escaped being benighted. Had they left a day later they must have inevitably run the gauntlet of being attacked and eaten by the packs of hungry wolves for which the forests were notorious. Even before the snow had fallen the wolves had started raiding the local villages, and killed several women and children, as well as two old men. They were like the nobles, the peasants said, robbers and assassins of the poor. But the youth feared the wolves far less than the peasants who had sworn when the party returned to the village to shoot both the landlord and his lovely daughter.

Then one evening a courier arrived in a sleigh, having travelled all night from St. Petersburg. When he announced that he brought news of the first importance he was at once admitted to the noble's presence. Some minutes later the latter summoned all the servants, and when they had assembled in the great hall, announced that the courier brought great news, for the Czar had decided that all the serfs were to be freed. The revelation was greeted with the wildest joy, and the youth's heart warmed with happiness until he remembered that owing to the snow no one would know about it back in the village. If his beloved mistress was not to be greeted on her return by a volley of shots there was only one thing to be done, and that was to go himself and inform the peasants.

Harnessing a sleigh the youth at once set out by the track leading through the forest to the village many versts away. Well aware that he ran the risk of having his horse pulled down by wolves he took a gun with him and plenty of ammunition. He had not gone far when he heard the wolves howling, and soon their green eyes were glistening in the starlight. The horse quickly scented the presence of its enemies, and putting back its ears galloped like a mad thing into the night. At first it appeared to outdistance its pursuers, but not for long. The pack followed relentlessly in its wake. The youth meantime abandoned the reins, and turned about to face the wolves. Soon the leader, a huge grey beast with a ruff on its neck as thick as that of a bear, came into range, and despite the rocking and slewing about of the vehicle, the youth nailed it with the first bullet. After pawing the air in agony it suddenly rolled over. At once the rest of the pack were worrying and fighting about the carcase, and by the time they had finished their cannibal meal the horse and its driver had drawn ahead. But the wolves were not to be so easily denied, and soon they came in view again, loping along as close as before.

By now their hungry howls had attracted the attention of other packs, and as the sleigh jolted through a clearing more wolves could be seen closing in from both flanks. Cursing in vexation, the youth swung round towards the new foes, and succeeded in dropping two of them before they could maim the horse. The beast, however, was tiring, and it was clear that the odds against survival were rapidly rising, and that the chase must inevitably end tragically. Determined to sell his life dearly, the brave young moujik continued to fire at the leaping shapes until his ammunition was exhausted. Suddenly ahead he glimpsed a light, and realized to his joy that it was the village. Urging the horse to make one last effort he drove the sleigh through the mansion gates, and into the carriage yard. The stable door was ajar, and the horse in its panic galloped headlong for it, and pulled up inside. Quick as thought the driver leaped out of the vehicle and speedily closed the doors. But he had reckoned without the pertinacity of the wolves which were still following hard at the horse's heels. Before he could retract his error seven wolves had dashed into the stable too. The villagers, alerted by the driver's cries, came running with guns to his assistance. The doors were reopened, and the wolves shot down as they cringed like cravens against the walls. The horse, to everyone's amazement, was quite uninjured, for the shock of their incarceration had caused the wolves to forget their prey. Meantime the young hero lost no time in recounting the exciting news, and preserving his master and mistress from a miserable fate.

Such is the kind of tale with which everyone is familiar, and although the details cannot be checked there is no reason to doubt that in the main it is true. Probably, however, such occasions were rare because in a land where wolves were common, neither lord nor peasant would have normally indulged, except in time of peril, in a midnight sleigh drive through the forest. At the same time many travellers must have been inevitably benighted and suffered the extreme penalty when attacked by hungry packs. Russian wolves are on the whole far larger and fiercer than their western counterparts, and approach in size the giants of Alaska which are larger and heavier than any breed of dog in the world. They are again far greyer in hue, and their heavy winter pelts give them a semi bear-like appearance, which makes them when roused and bristling seem even bigger than they are. During the cruel Russian winters they become famished, and then neither man nor village is safe.

The winter of 1927 was exceptionally severe, and round about Christmas a report reached the villages that droves of hungry wolves were moving westward from Siberia in search of food. The first sign of their presence was the disappearance of the watch-dogs. It might have been supposed that these formidable animals could have more than held their own in any encounter, but no dog is a match for a hungry wolf when suddenly surprised under cover of darkness. The dogs' remains were usually discovered far from the homesteads, for wolves prefer to drag their prey to the forest before eating it. Soon small children were missing too, and finally young women. Panic seized the villagers, for with blizzards raging they had no defence against the grey marauders. Very few wolves were shot or destroyed because they attacked only at night and retired to the forests during the daytime where, owing to the snow, the hunters were unable to follow them. As the weather worsened, success, as ever, rendered the beasts bolder, and soon no peasant was safe even in broad daylight.

When the rumours of the killings reached the village of Pilovo no one at first paid much heed. The harvest had failed, and less than ten years after the Revolution the peasants were finding it a hard enough task to remain alive in the near famine conditions. The cold was so intense that they remained for the most part in their huts, huddled about the stove. The only reason for going out was to search for fuel along the forest edge. Then one evening a forager failed to return. Fearing that he might have collapsed in the cold, his two brothers followed in his foot-prints as far as the trees, only to be seen no more themselves. Three more set out, but only one came back, trembling and retching with horror. As they had reached the forest they had been met by six wolves, which immediately pulled two of them down. The survivor had run for his life while the savage beasts mangled and tore his companions to pieces.

The villagers at once set up barricades, and it was well that they did so, for scarcely had the sun gone down than the howls of a hungry pack of wolves echoed through the narrow streets. As the peasants crouched fearfully round the stoves they could hear the horses and watch-dogs screaming with agony as their pitiless assailants attacked them. More terrifying still was the glimpse of grey snouts snuffing hungrily under the doors. At first in most cases the latter stood firm, for the peasants had set tables or beds against them, but the cottages belonging to two old women who lived alone were quickly invaded and the women were overpowered. Fear becomes tangible and soon communicates itself to wild beasts, and it did not take the wolves long to realize that they held the upper hand. So, no longer content with sniffing, they leaped boldly at the entrances, stood on their hind legs and used their paws as battering rams. Whenever the doors gave way the wolves flew in, and by morning had wrought a terrible toll.

Imagining that by then they would have returned to the forest, some of the bolder men ventured outside, but with the dogs dead and eaten there was no one any longer to warn or protect them, and before they realized the danger they too were doomed. For the first time in living memory an entire village was under siege, and for once not by human armies, but by regiments of ferocious beasts, for the triumphant howls of the original invaders had soon attracted others out of the forest so that hordes of hungry wolves were converging on Pilovo.

The terror of the helpless inhabitants may well be imagined. Cut off as they were in the best of times from the rest of the civilized world it would have been difficult enough to despatch a message through the snow even without the wolves. But now they were manifestly fated to die a death even more horrible than starvation, for to leave their huts to seek food or fuel was to incur the risk of being killed and eaten.

They were saved by a million to one chance. A military aeroplane had taken off despite the weather on a routine patrol of the regions adjacent to the Siberian border. It was probably scouting for signs of refugees, or even for foreign invaders. While crossing the desolate steppes around Ienisseik the pilot's attention was attracted by a pack of large dogs moving towards the frontier. That shepherds should be out in such weather and during the winter season was unthinkable. Besides there were no signs either of men or sheep. A few miles to the east more dogs appeared, moving in the same direction, so the pilot came down to have a closer look. Before he could give vent to his own suspicions his companion shouted, "Wolves!" Never in their young lives had the two airmen beheld such a sinister assembly, and one, moreover, which seemed to be converging, as far as they could judge, on one heavily forested village. Soon the wolves disappeared among the trees, but others arrived from the direction of the steppes. The roar of the engines brought the villagers to their doors, but even as they waved in desperation the horrified airmen observed grey shadows moving among the dwellings. Wheeling about they returned to their base and reported the wolf invasion.

The governor of Ienisseik immediately alerted the military forces under his command, and sent two detachments of Guards to relieve the beleaguered village. As they approached the scene of the disaster the soldiers could hear the young wolves howling, and it was not long before they encountered the first savage beasts. Deploying as if engaged in a military operation they began systematically to shoot the wolves down. The beasts soon realized that the odds were against them, and slowly withdrew towards the shelter of the forest. The scene of desolation which greeted the Guards when they entered the village was soul-searing to a degree. Hardly a family remained which had not suffered a loss, and the experience had rendered the survivors half demented. Most heart-rending of all were the poor little children who had seen a beloved parent devoured before their eyes.

The invasion was clearly on a notable scale for just a year later hordes of hungry wolves were observed crossing the plains of Hungary and Czecho-Slovakia. The beasts had not been seen for many years in these regions, and their sudden appearance caused wide-spread panic. Official warnings were issued to parents counselling them to keep their children indoors, and to barricade themselves against possible invasion. In the meantime the packs moved on across the frozen rivers into western Europe, for once again they had the weather on their side and were not halted by natural conditions. Inevitably tragedies occurred. Farmers, ignorant of the insidious ways of wolves, neglected to close byres or sheds, and were lucky if they lost only their dogs or stock and not their women or children. Then came news whose horror thrilled the world. Eleven young girls from the village of Marmaras-Sziget, which is situated near the foot of the Carpathian mountains, were passing through a forest when they were suddenly surprised by wolves. Shrieking in terror the girls scattered like sheep in all directions. And as though they had been sheep the wolves attacked them, snapping mouthfuls of living flesh from their screaming victims or cruelly mangling them on the ground. Soon none was left alive to tell the story of those dreadful moments, and the pack settled down to its ghoulish feast. This and similar events must inevitably test the faith of Christians in a deity who can permit such horrors to be. Indeed at times the wolf seems to become the living embodiment of the powers of darkness striking down the innocent and preying on the weak.

In 1914 a caravan was crossing the steppes near the Ural mountains. The latter, of course, were and still are notorious for wild beasts including large and fearsome bears. But the caravan was large and no danger was feared either from these or from wolves. It consisted in the main of sturdy ponies and horsemen, carts filled with handsome high-cheeked Cossack women and their grave Mongol-eyed children, and a few camels laden with merchandise. Dogs patrolled the flanks as the convoy jolted forward, while armed men rode at the front and rear. These precautions were considered necessary against possible bandit raids, and the attempts of wolves under cover of darkness to make off with the odd goat or sheep.

Then one night the members of the caravan were roused by the sound of wolves howling on the outskirts of the encampment. The dogs barked hysterically in defiance of their foes, while the women and children huddled closer over the fires. The guards on duty were soon alarmed by the number of red eyes reflecting the glow, for instead of a pack of six or seven wolves they seemed to be surrounded by fifty. In fact an invasion of thirty beasts had suddenly converged on the travellers. The steppes were uninhabited and the scent of the cooking soon roused the neighbouring packs. Sensing the convoy's predicament in the darkness the beasts moved in close to the carts. The dogs presented no difficulty to wolves in such numbers, while the guards were afraid to fire for fear of wounding their families. Though a wolf is incapable of rational thought it possesses an uncanny knack of summing up the strength and weakness of a situation to a wholly remarkable degree. At any rate, before the watch was fully cognizant of what was happening the grey shadows were moving swiftly round the tents, and boldly attacking the women and children. Even the fires failed to deter them, and instead of retreating the wolves began to snatch their victims from alongside the flames. When the men rushed back clubbing their rifles the leaders lay in ambush and pulled them down. Soon all was silent apart from the groans of dying children, and the terrified bleats of stampeding sheep. That night the wolves of the Urals feasted royally, and when a search party finally lighted on the convoy only the carts were intact. The rest was a litter of mangled bones and blood-stained clothing. Even Attila at his worst could scarcely have wreaked greater havoc.

Later the same year when the ill-led and worse fed Russian armies moved across the border in the direction of Prussia the wolves, sensing battle and food for the taking, slunk in their rear on the look-out for prey. Many a lost soldier wandering in the forests was surprised and eaten, and few of those who fell in battle were left long in need of burial or of human help if still alive.

In Germany wolves have long been extinct, though during "invasion" years the beasts overrun her borders. Formerly they were exceedingly common, and it is recorded that no less than six thousand were hunted and killed by the electors of Saxony during the seventeenth century. Their numbers increased again during the period of the Napoleonic Wars, and only poison proved effective against them in the province of Posen. Later, during the revolutionary era of 1831 to 1836 wolves invaded Prussia again from Poland, and 256 were recorded as slain. Thereafter they became rare again until the outbreak of the Franco-Prussian War.

The wolf's powers of recuperation is generally evident after a great war, when their presence tends to pass unnoticed, and there is no one to hunt them even when it is. The huge cataclysm which rocked France yet again to her foundations, and seriously disturbed the eastern borders offered the wolves the kind of chance that they had formerly enjoyed during the days of the Revolution, and the province of Alsace-Lorraine was quickly invaded. Vigorous measures were taken to protect the populace, and the incredible number of 2,500 wolves were destroyed.

Where such vast assemblages originally derived from is a problem for naturalists, though it is generally supposed that they came from Poland. Certainly they were common enough there during the nineteenth century, though hardly on the scale which such figures might have been supposed to imply. Four young girls were killed and eaten in 1837, oddly enough in August, for wolves are endlessly on the prowl, and though rendered more daring by the pinch of winter they are prepared to attack the weakly at any time whether animal or human. Forty wolves were killed in 1870 in the great primeval forest of Bialowieza, and sixty-three in the following year. But in 1891 only six were recorded as having been destroyed, although it was still computed in 1929 that two thousand survived in the forests of Poland. Obviously all the wolves in Poland did not suddenly invade Alsace-Lorraine, and the conclusion seems inevitable that the beasts came from further east.

The evidence from Siberia already mentioned might seem to suggest that wolf movements are activated much like those of men, and that pressure from afar pushes all the packs westward. The vast steppes of Mongolia still harbour innumerable wolves, against whose continual assaults even in broad daylight the nomad shepherds are comparatively helpless. As there is no cover the shepherds' sole defence is to ring their flocks with savage dogs. But even these rarely deter the wolves which prowl incessantly round the canine sentries waiting for an opportunity to seize a lamb. When the wolves work in pairs or packs the dogs' attention is deliberately diverted by the approach of one beast while the others make off with the prey. Scuffles and fights are of incessant occurrence, and at night in particular many dogs are destroyed. During the kind of arctic winters that the steppes sometimes know, when the flocks are folded or buried in the drifts, it seems inevitable that the packs should move westward driving their hungry brethren ahead. As wolves are capable of travelling enormous distances in a remarkably short time it is scarcely surprising that they should suddenly appear in areas where they were long believed extinct, far remote from their normal haunts.

Of course no one knows just how many wolves inhabit any given forest, but there is reason to suppose that they rarely overpopulate any region, as each pack demands *lebensraum*. So once the wolf population has outgrown its hunting area, the younger members are persuaded, none too kindly, to move on and occupy adjacent territory. This again would doubtless constitute a contributory factor, though it would hardly account for movements on a large scale. Thus under favourable circumstances wolves could reappear in parts of France and Italy, where they had been extinct for many years. Indeed the presence of wolves has been noted in the forest of Fontainebleau during exceptional winters within only a few kilometres of Paris. How even that famous capital was invaded during the civil wars at the beginning of the fifteenth century has already been described. Then shepherds were attacked in what is now Montmartre, and the hungry beasts fed on the dead festering in the streets. The awful sound of wolves howling must have been all too familiar to the famine-stricken citizens cowering in their houses. Even today it is exciting to realize that wolf-routes still lie open between Poland and France. That during severe winters wolves cross the frozen river barriers separating western from eastern Europe has been proved over and over again.

At the same time it is hard to believe that the wolves seen in Vienne and Charente during recent years arrived from this direction. Probably remnants of former indigenous packs still survive in the fastnesses of the great forests of the south-western districts, and are occasionally reinforced by wolves from Spain. Even so, the possibility of the existence of a primeval wolf-route leading from central Europe cannot positively be ruled out, and at any rate that seems to be the view of the local peasants.

That wolves are still very much in the habit of invading adjacent territories appears to be borne out by recent Finnish experience. The vast forests on Finland's eastern borders seem well designed as a refuge for wolves. But there, as elsewhere, every man's hand is turned against them, and any wolf that is seen is ruthlessly shot down. Even so the scale of the annual winter invasions is sometimes claimed to be such that escorts are required to protect children walking to school.

Poland, too, is a frequent sufferer from wolves. Though the beasts are indigenous and are still found in great numbers throughout the eastern provinces, there are in addition periodic invasions from Russia. The Russian wolves are believed to follow two main routes, one running due west across the provinces of Bialystok and Olszlyn, while the second crosses Rzeszow in the south-east. Both routes are now watched by hunters, but the main invasions naturally tend to occur during hard winters when observation is most difficult. As a consequence many wolves continue to get through and ravage the countryside beyond. Government action has proved effective, but it is interesting to learn that there is no present intention to exterminate wolves, only to keep them under rigorous control. Whether, in fact, this desirable aim is possible in the case of an animal so cunning and ferocious seems doubtful, for unlike other beasts the great carnivora cannot be herded into reserves and the safety of wolves could hardly be guaranteed even though they were confined in an area surrounded by high walls. Inevitably a tree would collapse one day and provide them with a bridge across, or the wall would be breached in a storm. In countries again so thickly forested as Russia and Poland control is rendered doubly difficult, particularly when in the former case the way lies open to invasion from the steppes. It will be interesting to see how long the wolf survives within the Soviet Union. The pointers are that it will not be exterminated for many years.

The biggest wolves in the world are found in Alaska, where they frequently attain a length of six feet, and a weight upwards of ten stone. Their prey is the caribou, the wild reindeer, which roams the northern tundras in enormous herds. Meat is so plentiful that they seldom attack human beings, except on the rare occasions when they become rabid. Helge Instad describes in *Nunamiut* how one evening an Eskimo hunter was awakened by a furious disturbance among the dogs. Seizing his gun he dashed outside to investigate and found all the animals struggling and fighting in a snarling mass. Suddenly a huge grey beast detached itself from the milling throng and leaped fiercely at his throat. Fortunately his reactions were abnormally fast and he managed to shoot it dead.

On examination the wolf proved to be rabid, and next morning two dogs died of hydrophobia. Had the hunter gone unarmed he must have paid the awful penalty familiar through examples from Russia and France. Yet some Eskimos survived attacks unscathed, and the hunter's father was a case in point. One day he had gone out to watch caribou, and while observing the distant herd a wolf attacked him. He was squatting on a hillock at the time when the beast knocked him over and bit his anorak to pieces. Having neither gun nor knife about him the old Eskimo vigorously defended himself with his stick, and in the end the wolf had enough and left its victim wounded but alive. That the beast was rabid was apparent from the foam on its jaws, yet the wounds healed in time and the old man was no worse for his unnerving adventure.

A recent case of a wolf attacking a human being was recorded in *Pulse* on 2nd January 1963. A farmer named Isidore Carre from Northern Ontario was bitten in the neck by a member of a pack raiding in the area. Whether or not the wolf was rabid had not been ascertained at the time when the notice appeared, but precautions had been taken, and so far Mr. Carre was reported as being in good health.

The love of wolves for caribou was perhaps insufficiently appreciated by those responsible for attempts to introduce domestic reindeer into Alaska. During the ten years between 1892 and 1902 no less than 1,280 reindeer were transferred from Siberia to the coastal areas of northern and north-western Alaska, and Lapps arrived from Norway to help get them established. At first the herds did well, and it was estimated in 1930 that they numbered half a million. But owing to imperfect supervision by the Eskimos or their sponsors some became feral while others died. Meantime the wolves got busy, and severely decimated the remainder. Yet despite these handicaps a fresh attempt has been made with Government backing to render the Eskimos reindeer conscious, and forty thousand beasts are now said to be in existence and thriving despite the wolves. Fortunately there is plenty of caribou left, and the wolves are rarely tempted to attack the domestic herds. Indeed, even in Europe wolves are said to prefer a diet of deer, if it is available, to that of cattle or sheep. Horses, however, are always in danger, for their flesh has a peculiar attraction for carnivora which in past ages hunted horses in the wild.

With so much game to eat the wolves of Alaska are rarely driven to attack men, and when they do so it is sometimes by mistake. Helge Instad describes how an Eskimo hunter was once crawling towards some caribou on a misty day when something heavy landed on his back and sharp fangs sank into his arm. The wolf had apparently mistaken the hunter for a caribou calf, but quickly retreated when it discovered its mistake.

*Chapter Thirteen*

# The Wolf in Legend

ONE day many years ago in Auvergne, the hilly region of southern France where wolves were formerly common, a gentleman was seated at an open window in the cool of the evening admiring the magnificent prospect of forest, mountains and streams. Suddenly he observed a friend of his going out to hunt. Hailing him cheerily he begged him to bring him back some of his bag, and the hunter gladly assented. The hunter was after hares or deer, and was therefore somewhat disconcerted when he met instead an enormous wolf. Levelling his musket he fired at the beast, but the shot inexplicably went wide. The wolf thereupon attacked him, but as it closed he managed to draw his knife. After a tremendous struggle he succeeded in severing its right fore-paw, whereupon the wolf immediately fled.

When he at last returned, the gentleman inquired whether he had had any luck. He replied ruefully in the negative, but added the jocular remark that if a wolf's paw was any good to him he was quite welcome to have it. His friend expressed a wish to see it, so after describing the encounter he drew the bleeding trophy from his bag. His horror may be imagined when he discovered on doing so that the paw had changed mysteriously into a woman's hand, with a gold ring on one of the fingers. Uttering a startled exclamation the gentleman turned ghastly pale, for he had recognized the ring as belonging to his wife. He at once hurried home to confront her with the evidence, and found her drowsing before the fire with her right arm hidden beneath her apron.

"Ah, *loup-garou*," he shouted, "put forth your arm so that I may see for myself how you pass your time!"

The woman at first refused, but when her outraged husband produced the hand, she suddenly broke down and displayed the bleeding stump. The hand fitted perfectly and the woman duly confessed that she had been a werewolf for several years. Her husband at once handed her over to the civil authorities and she was duly burned as a witch. How far the tale has been embroidered one may only surmise, but the records ascribe the burning to the year 1588.

Some years earlier, in 1521, two men were arraigned on a charge of being werewolves before the Dominicans of Poligny in the diocese of Alençon. One of them, Pierre Burgot, alleged that many years before his cattle had strayed, and that a black cavalier had herded them together after he had agreed to give himself to his master, the Devil. Later the other defendant, called Michel Verdun, had taught him at the Witches' Sabbath how to become a werewolf by rubbing himself with a certain ointment. When he had done so his limbs were turned into paws and hair grew over his body. He could, moreover, run like the wind, and had to all appearances become a wolf. Verdun also transformed himself in the same way through the medium of the ointment which he claimed to have obtained from his demon master. In the form of wolves they killed several children, sucked their blood and ate part of their flesh. Burgot also confessed, to the monks' horror, that he had frequently indulged in sexual relations with wolves. Both were burned alive on their own admission.

At the same time three other sorcerers were executed for the same crime on the evidence of a hunter. The latter, it appeared, had wounded a wolf and followed it through the forest. The blood trail led to a hut, and when he went in to destroy the beast he found a peasant having a wound dressed by his wife. Probably the matter was pure coincidence and the hunter had confused two blood trails, one belonging to the wolf, and the other to the peasant who had injured himself with a tool. But in an era of superstition the evidence was deemed conclusive, and the wretch was at once condemned to die.

A similar charge was brought against a certain hermit of Lyons who had found life too irksome and taken a concubine. The couple lived in dire poverty with their children, and presumably would never had been heard of save for a certain event. About that time a large wolf appeared in the neighbourhood and the bodies of several children were found half-eaten. Then another boy was attacked. His cries brought assistance, but by then it was too late though the hermit was found bending over the body. He was at once accused of being a werewolf and at his trial at Dôle he confessed to being a wolf, adding the information that he had sold himself to the Devil, and transformed himself into beast form by anointing himself with ointment. He had killed and eaten the children, he said, and his consort had shared in the meal. He too was burned alive, the proper punishment for werewolves as laid down by religious decree.

A certain Jacques Rollet was arrested at Condé in 1598 on the charge of being a *loup-garou*. It appeared that a child had been killed and two wolves had been seen feeding on his carcase. A third ran off into a neighbouring field where a man of wild appearance was hiding. When accused he confessed to being a wolf, and stated that the two beasts were his brother and cousin, who had helped him kill the child and shared the hideous feast. At his trial he maintained that he had acquired the power of changing himself into a wolf by using a certain ointment. He was sentenced to death, but the verdict was overruled by the Parlement of Paris on the grounds that he was unfit to plead. It seems strange at such a period, when superstitious and religious beliefs were apt to oust all other considerations, that the unhinged state of mind of the poverty-stricken creature was finally given due weight. Instead of being burned he was confined in a hospital for the rest of his days. Whether he was, in fact, technically guilty of cannibalism is hard to say, though it is difficult to believe that even such an abject wretch would have actually murdered a child in order to relieve his hunger.

Whatever the truth in individual cases, European literature abounds in stories about werewolves—i.e. men who were credited with the power of assuming wolf form. Indeed the belief in lycanthropy was familiar to the ancients, and is still found among the inhabitants of the more backward areas of Spain, France, Italy, and further east even today. The following is a typical French tale.

During the last century a farmer was mystified by the long absences of one of his employees during the hours of darkness, and in the end he was obliged to come to the conclusion that he never slept at all. What was even more strange was that his disappearances invariably coincided with the arrival of a wolf, which used to rouse the dogs to madness by sniffing through the cat-hole under the main gate. Soon the neighbours began to talk. The man was a *loup-garou,* they said, who changed himself into a wolf at night and prowled round the steadings. The farmer, suspecting that if accused to his face the labourer would deny the charge, decided to follow him and discover where he went. The man walked to a hut and, after stripping to the buff, buckled round his waist a long thin belt. The moment he had completed this operation he changed into a wolf, and slipped away like a shadow into the night. Running back to the farm his master armed himself with a stick, and then sat up to wait for him beside the cat-hole. The vigil was a long one, and he was on the point of falling asleep when the dogs in the rick-yard set up a furious barking. Leaping to his feet he observed a lean grey muzzle sniffing hungrily through the slot. The stick descended, but instead of a howl of pain a human voice reached the farmer's ears.

"Thank heaven!" it cried. "I still had three years to go!" Needless to say when the man returned to work next morning he sported a bloody nose. But as the spell had been broken no one took any action, and the wolf's visits ended less mysteriously than they had begun.

One of the ways in which a werewolf could be detected was by wounding it in wolf-form and then searching for a human being with similar wounds. This led to the previously described unmasking of the witch-wife of Auvergne, and was applied in Padua with even more extraordinary effect. Apparently a wolf was in the habit of roaming through the streets at night, an occurrence not unknown in Italy and indeed reported during the winter of 1963 from no less a city than Rome. Its presence alarmed the populace, and many attempts were made to capture or slay it, but at first without success. Meanwhile a reign of terror went on until the citizens became desperate. The aid of an experienced hunter was sought, and he quickly realized that the beast in question was one of no ordinary cunning. Nevertheless, its sheer delight in killing eventually proved its undoing, and one day it fell into a trap. Guessing that it was a werewolf the hunter at once severed its paws, as it was everywhere believed that they were, as McQueen says, "Very precarious creatures." To the observers' shocked amazement the beast at once reassumed the form of a man minus hands and feet.

In a German tale a woman told her husband to throw his hat at any beast that came. Later a wolf appeared among the hay makers, and a boy managed to stab it with a fork. The beast then changed into a woman who was already dead, and was in fact the man's wife. Here one cannot help wondering whether the boy did not kill the woman by mistake in the heat of the moment, and used the legend to disguise his error—that is always assuming that the tale held truth.

According to a Dutch story, a man saw a wolf attacking a girl and fired an arrow at it. The wolf ran off with the arrow sticking in its side and howling piteously. Next day news reached the archer that a serving man lay dying with an arrow in his side. When he went to investigate he found, as he suspected, that the arrow was his, whereupon the man confessed that he was a werewolf.

One day in Denmark a man was sitting with his wife when he suddenly realized as on many previous occasions, that he was on the point of changing into a wolf. Bidding her strike with her apron anything which approached he quickly ran off. Soon a wolf appeared, and after biting a piece from the apron swiftly went away. Subsequently the man returned carrying the cloth and explained to his wife that he was now at last free of the spell. Such stories undoubtedly contain some element of the strange aberration know as wolf-madness which is recognized as a form of dementia.

The belief that a human being can assume wolf form by wearing a strap made out of wolf's skin is found in Germany as well as France. The period of transformation varied but was usually given as seven years, or alternatively as many days, months or years as the hole used in the buckle. The cycle could only be broken if the werewolf were wounded in animal form, or struck by some object like an apron or a hat.

In Armenia wicked women are supposed to don wolf-skins and become werewolves for seven years. They devour their children first, then those of their relations and finally strangers' too. They invade houses at night, and drop their skins in the morning when they return to human form. If the skin is discovered and destroyed the women suffer agonies and finally perish.

Werewolf stories are rare in England and Scotland. Drayton, however, recounts a legend about a man who changed himself into a wolf by eating certain herbs under certain specified conditions. Subsequently he committed great havoc among the sheep, and finally attacked an ass. Unfortunately for the werewolf the ass also was a human being transformed, and the latter roused the people to slay him.

In Ireland, however, as wolves lingered longer, so did the legends about them. Giraldus Cambrensis, who visited Ireland during the time of King John, tells how a priest once met a wolf in Meath which begged him to visit his dying wife. Both were apparently natives of Ossory whose people had been cursed for their wickedness by Saint Natalis and been compelled to take wolf form in turn for a period of seven years. The priest was persuaded to follow the beast to a place where its mate lay dying. At first the holy man was unconvinced that the sick wolf was in fact a woman, so her husband rolled down a bit of skin and showed that she was really human.

It was a common belief that the people of Ossory possessed the power of becoming werewolves and went out to devour their fellows, and St. Patrick himself is said to have visited certain sinners with this fell power. That the source of this belief was ultimately totemistic has been suggested by many authorities, and this might explain the statements by English travellers that the Irish took wolves as their godfathers, prayed to them not to do them ill, and used their teeth as charms. Again the circumstance that lycanthropy was believed to run in families suggests a totem origin.

In Slavonic countries werewolves were credited with supernatural powers such as the ability to cause eclipses. A person who possessed this power was supposed to have had a wolf as father and to have been born feet first. Though the upper part of his body resembled a human being his lower half suggested the wolf, and he had a wolf's heart and teeth. In order to become a wolf all that was necessary was to drink some water from a wolf's footprint, or turn over a fallen tree and don a wolfskin. Among the Jugoslavs it was believed that werewolves held gatherings and hung their skins on trees. As in Armenia, if these skins were found and destroyed the werewolves lost their magic powers.

There is a Polish story that a wolf seized a girl at a merrymaking and carried her off into the forest. Such events sometimes occurred, as we know from France, but in this case there was an unusual sequence. Many years later a peasant met the girl's long-lost brother. The latter was a man of wild appearance who had disappeared from the district in his youth, it was believed after committing some crime. In the course of conversation the tragedy which had befallen the girl was mentioned at which her brother began to look uncomfortable. In the end he confessed that he had been the wolf in question, and that his aim had been to persuade his sister to become a werewolf too. But she had pined and died, and in his bitter grief he had attacked and killed many human beings. Now he had returned briefly to see his home once more before returning to the forest. The peasant accompanied him as far as the cottage and then was horrified to see him become a wolf again.

Werewolves, it seems, were subject to human feelings, and could be as jealous as anyone else. A married man gained the power of becoming a wolf and one day ran off into the forest. What had happened to him no one could guess, least of all his young wife who was naturally grief-stricken. In time, however, she got over her loss and, as it was commonly assumed that her husband was dead, she married a neighbouring peasant. The marriage was happy and in the course of time the woman gave birth to children. Then one night there came a loud knock at the door. The woman went to see who it was and almost fainted when she recognized her first husband. His hair was unkempt, his clothes were in rags and his eyes held a savage gleam.

"I have come home, good wife," he growled. "Prepare me a bowl of cabbage."

At that moment the woman's second husband entered, bearing a log, and ordered the stranger to leave. At first the latter could not be made to understand that the woman was no longer his wife, so at last she produced the children. Gazing at them wildly the former husband shouted, "Oh, would that I might become a wolf again in order to punish this woman!" His wish was granted, and with a bestial howl he leaped upon the children. The woman's screams brought the neighbours flying, armed with hatchets, but by the time they had arrived all the children were dead. The wolf was soon despatched, but as it died it became a man once more.

One day a witch lay in wait for a bridal party, for it was a common belief that women were must susceptible to evil influences when in the process of getting married. First twisting her girdle, for knots contain evil, the witch laid it across the threshold of the house where the wedding was being celebrated, so that the bride and bridegroom would be obliged to step over it and so come into her power. In due course they did so, with the bridal party in attendance, and in a moment were changed into wolves. They all ran away into the forest, but returned every night in order to give the witch satisfaction by howling around her cottage. She had fixed the term of their bestial incarnation at seven years, and at the end of that period they reassumed human shape. This the witch accomplished by the simple expedient of covering them with wolfskins turned inside out. Unfortunately the bridegroom was a tall man, and the skin proved too short to cover his whole body, so he was doomed to wear a wolf's tail for the remainder of his life!

In France werewolves could be distinguished by this very feature which was always truncated, and never bushy or long. They could also be forced to reassume human form by binding them with a strap of human hair, if indeed this difficult operation could be accomplished. As werewolves were believed to strip naked before assuming wolf form, their subsequent reconversion could be prevented by removing their clothes. This in effect was a variation of the theme of confiscating the wolf skin which a werewolf was supposed to assume.

The superstition that a werewolf had first to strip is very old and is effectively described by Petronius. One of the guests at Trimalchio's feast tells how in his youth he fell in love with an innkeeper's wife. His passion was returned, and when the lady's husband died he decided to go and visit her. For company on the journey he took a soldier, a neighbour of his, who feared nothing and was "as strong as Death himself." The pair set out at cock-crow while the moon was still shining, and eventually reached a graveyard beside the road. The soldier immediately made for the tombs, while his companion beguiled the time by singing and counting their number. When he chanced to glance round he observed the soldier taking off his clothes. But if this proceeding were sufficiently extraordinary the next was infinitely more so. After micturating round them he laid them in a heap by the roadside. His friend watched in mounting horror as he changed himself into a wolf and ran howling into the forest. At first he imagined he must be dreaming, and went to have a closer look at the clothes. But a further shock awaited him for instead of a pile of linen he found a heap of stones. He almost expired with fright, and drawing his sword made passes at every lurking shadow all the way to the lady's house. When he finally arrived, looking like a ghost and half-blinded by fear and sweat, the widow chided him for being so late.

"If you'd only come before," she said, "you could have done some good." Then she went on to describe how a wolf had entered the farm and turned the cow-shed into a shambles. She, however, claimed to have had the last laugh even though the beast got away, for a slave she had summoned to her assistance had speared it in the neck.

The lover was too tired to do anything about it just then but next morning he set out for his master's house, determined to solve the mystery. When he reached the place where the clothes had been transformed into stone he found a tell-tale pool of blood.

When he eventually arrived home inquiries respecting the soldier's whereabouts revealed that he had suffered an accident and been confined to bed with a doctor in attendance. Convinced by the proof that his friend was a werewolf he confessed to the company that he could never bring himself afterwards to share a meal with him even if his life had depended on it.

The scientifically-minded elder Pliny was shocked by such rank superstitions. "That men can be changed into wolves," he writes, "and back again I shall dismiss here and now as rubbish. Otherwise we should have to accept all the stories which our extensive researches have proved to be false." He then proceeds to quote the Arcadian tradition that men could become wolves by following a certain procedure. After being chosen by lot the candidate for initiation was brought to a certain marsh, where he took off his clothes and hung them on an oak. He then swam across the swamp to the wild region beyond and consorted with the wolves as one of themselves. After living as a member of the pack for nine years he returned across the swamp, put on his clothes and became a man again. His safe return, however, depended on the important proviso that he should not, while in wolf form, have attacked a human being. Pliny comments dryly on the extent of Greek credulity which could believe that after nine years the man's clothes were still hanging on the tree! Nevertheless the proviso that he should not have attacked his fellows does look as though the purpose of the initiation was to deter the attacks of wolves.

The story also survives in the myth about Lycaon, the ferocious Arcadian cannibal-king, whose very name sounds like *lycos* (wolf). His misdeeds reached the ears of Zeus and the king of gods and men came down to earth to investigate the report in person. When he entered Lycaon's palace even the king's slaves seemed to sense that it was a god they were honouring, but their master decided to put his guest to the test. He first attempted to murder him while he was asleep, and when this plot miscarried traitorously slew a Molossian who was also staying in the house, and was therefore under Zeus' own protection in his capacity as *Xenios*—Guardian of Guests. Having killed him, the ghoulish monarch next boiled his flesh and served him up for the god to eat. This was too much even for the almighty father's patience, and he destroyed the palace with a thunderbolt. Lycaon fled in terror, and when he gained the open country burst into howls, and in his mad blood-lust attacked the flocks. Thereupon his clothes turned into shaggy fur, and his arms into legs. In short he became a wolf, the creature he had so closely resembled as a man, and the only tokens which he retained of his previous shape were the same grey colour, lawless mien, fierce gleam in the eye and general longing for savagery. The story of Lycaon is explained as a mythological description of a ritual held in honour of Zeus Lycaeus on Mount Lycaeum in Arcadia. According to the ancient authorities the festival took place every ninth year when transformation into wolf form was achieved by tasting a dish compounded of the bowels of humans and animals. The latter, of course, was typical wolf fare and was doubtless selected for that very reason. The purpose of the transformation is perhaps not difficult to arrive at. Doubtless wolves were a major pest in old times in Arcadia, and the aim would have been to placate them. Certainly there was a curious parallel in modern France. It was the custom of priests at Périgord, a district where wolves were common, to rush to the local fountains when the moon was full, and plunge incontinent into the water. They emerged wearing goat skins, and rushed about on all fours attacking men and animals. At the end of the performance they plunged in afresh emerging as normal human beings.

There is also a marked analogy with the hideous leopard secret societies of West Africa, the members of which wear leopard skins and sharp steel claws. So accoutred they murder women by tearing off their breasts, and eat them in order to derive power from their bodies. While so engaged they clearly regard themselves as leopards, just as wolf-men believed that by ritual they had acquired the strength of wolves.

Wolf totems again undoubtedly contributed to a belief in lycanthropy, for when a tribe has adopted a wolf as its protective beast it is usual for the male members to seek initiation as wolves. This happened most frequently among the American Indians. At Nootka Sound the braves dressed up in wolfskins and wolf-masks, and after seizing the candidate for initiation carried him off into the forest. They behaved in fact precisely like their real counterparts while the novice fulfilled the role of a hunted beast. During the night the novice suffered ritual slaughter through the medium of a magic stone, and next day the wolf-men returned with his "corpse." They then set about reviving him by removing the stone, and at the end of the ceremony the novice was regarded as having become a wolf-man too.

Ritual death and rebirth is a common feature in primitive initiation ceremonies, and there is no reason to suppose that the participants did not regard themselves for the nonce as transformed into real wolves. This gave rise to the tradition that wolves had once made off with the chief's son, but having failed to kill him had decided to become his friends. Subsequently they had taught him the rites of their society, and commanded him in return to instruct the members of his tribe. When he agreed to do so they carried him back safely to the village. Some such ritual seems to underly the story of Lycaon, and also to Herodotus' reference to the practices of the Neurians. According to the father of history, every year a member of this Scythian tribe became a wolf for a few days and was subsequently restored to his proper shape. The historian expresses disbelief in the story, though the local Greeks and Scythians were prepared to stake their solemn oaths that it was perfectly true. Clearly it was true, though Herodotus was quite right to disbelieve in a real transformation. What happened was that the novice dressed up and behaved like a wolf during the period of his initiation into a wolf-society.

At Jumièges in Normandy there was formerly held on Midsummer's Eve a curious fire-festival. The celebrants, who were known as the Brotherhood of the Green Wolf, and wore hoods drawn down to their shoulders, then formally installed their new chief. On assuming office he donned a long green mantle, and a tall green hat without a brim. Marching at their head he led the way from his home village of Conihout to a place called Chouquet. As the procession moved along the brethren chanted the hymn of St. John the Baptist whose feast was to be celebrated on the following day. At Chouquet they were greeted by the local priest who conducted them to church. When Mass had been celebrated the celebrants returned to Conihout for refreshment at Green Wolf's house. Later they danced outside his door to the accompaniment of hand-bells rung by a village youth and maiden until the time came to light the bonfire. As the flames shot up the villagers chanted the Te Deum while Green Wolf and his brothers circled the fire holding hands in pursuit of Green Wolf's successor. The Green Wolf elect laid about him with a stick in his attempts to escape to the considerable diversion of the spectators. When he had been captured three times a pretence was made of hurling him on the bonfire. Finally the party returned to Green Wolf's house for supper, but were strictly charged to mind their speech. Censors were appointed armed with hand-bells who immediately interrupted the proceedings if anyone swore or said anything improper, and fined him on the spot. But on the stroke of midnight licence was declared and the Wolves celebrated St. John with ribald ditties. The fiddlers screeched and the entire assemblage abandoned itself to the wildest orgies. Next day further celebrations took place, including the production of a sacred loaf to the sound of a fusillade of muskets. Finally the hand-bells were deposited on the step of the church altar and entrusted to the Green Wolf elect as the insignia of his office.

Midsummer fire festivals are found the world over, but the origin of Green Wolf is lost in the mists of time. Certainly wolves were formerly very common in the Bocage in Normandy, and the beast was doubtless held in considerable fear. If you cannot overcome your enemy the next best thing is to make friends with him, and this presumably the Green Wolves attempted to do. There was also doubtless some connection with fertility festivals, as shown by the licence and the celebrants' garb. Green is the colour of nature as well as of the dresses of fairies, and Green Wolf was in some form a symbol of nature. The process by which he became a wolf we shall never know, though the beasts' depredations may well have been responsible for the type of mummery chosen.

The ancient Greeks were also troubled by wolves, and turned for protection to the god of plagues. Whether Apollo Lykeios was originally so called because he was in fact a wolf (lykos)—god, or whether it was because he originally hailed from Lycia has been hotly disputed. His worshippers, at any rate, clearly believed in his "wolfish" aspect on the reasonable grounds that a god who was responsible for plagues, whether of wolves or field-mice, was obviously best suited to take them away. Indeed there was an old story that

Athens herself was once infested by wolves. The tradition is, of course, not impossible, as the beasts formerly roamed the hills of Attica, and during hard seasons must have wandered down into the city. At any rate, when the citizens appealed to Apollo the god ordered them to offer sacrifices at the Lyceum, where Aristotle taught later, which meant in Greek "the place of wolves." The beasts were then said to have been destroyed by the smell of the sacrifices, instead of being attracted as one might have supposed. So at Sicyon, on the Gulf of Corinth, when the wolves descended from the mountains of Achaea and decimated the flocks, Apollo instructed the shepherds to put out baits of meat which at once proved fatal.

Whether these legends are a record of early attempts to destroy wolves by poison, or whether the meals were intended to buy them off is uncertain. It may at least be mentioned that when a lion became troublesome to a farmer in Kenya the provision of free feeds was received in the spirit in which it was tendered and the farmer's horses remained unscathed.

Apollo was also worshipped as a wolf-god in ancient Italy on Mount Soracte, where his worshippers were known as "hirpi" (the old Sabine name for wolves) and dressed up in wolfskins precisely like Red Indians.

When Julius Caesar married the young Calpurnia he did so mainly in the hope of having a son. But Calpurnia remained barren, and in Shakespeare's play the great dictator charges her to stand in Mark Antony's way during the celebration of the Lupercalia—the feast of the Wolfish Pan. This, perhaps the oldest of all Roman festivals was held on 15th February and celebrated by the Luperci. The Luperci, whose name seems to mean "warders off of wolves," belonged to two prominent colleges to which Caesar added a third. The rites were associated with the Palatine hill in Rome and were probably of immemorial antiquity. After assembling at the cave where Romulus and Remus were said to have been suckled by the she-wolf, the Luperci offered sacrifices of goats and dogs to the rustic deity Faunus, who was identified with the Greek god Pan. Goats of course represented the flocks to be protected, while dogs were often offered to underworld powers. Next two young men of good family had their heads smeared with blood from the victims, and then wiped with wool dipped in milk. They were then expected to laugh as if reborn after suffering ritual sacrifice. Girdling themselves with the skins of the sacrificed goats the celebrants then feasted. Later they ran down from the Palatine waving tawses made of goatskin and beat all the women in order to make them fertile. Antony took part because he had been elected master of the new lodge created by Caesar.

The rite is hard to unravel in its entirety, but seems to be composed of several elements. Originally we may suppose that the Luperci were, as their name implies, protectors of flocks from the wolves. The fact that they wore skins supports this contention though they were admittedly not those of their totem. The initiation of the youths is in essence similar to that performed by savage tribes, and to the rites performed in honour of Zeus Lycaeus. Indeed it was supposed that Faunus was identical with the Lycean Pan, who was also a deity who protected and prospered the flocks in Arcadia. The beatings too are reminiscent of the old custom of beating the image of Pan with squills in order to promote fertility. Clearly what had originally been a simple rustic rite to ward off the assaults of wolves had as Rome grew extended its sphere of influence to include the promotion of fertility among the entire populace. The myth of Lycaon suggests human sacrifice, and according to one version of the legend a child was sacrificed to Zeus. This then seems to have its counterpart in the bloody smearing of initiates who were originally victims.

Sacrifice to wolves was not confined to the ancients, for down to the seventeenth century the Letts were in the habit of offering a goat to the wolves in the hope that they would henceforth spare their flocks. The sacrifice was made at the witching time of Christmas, as the beasts were popularly supposed to be at their most dangerous between the 25th December and Twelfth Night. It was performed at a cross-roads, a spot singularly appropriate for the celebration of the black arts, with full pagan rites. When it was over the celebrants boasted loudly that their beasts were immune for the rest of the year, even though a whole pack of wolves ran through their herds. By such a combination of propitiation and boldness they believed they could influence the bloodthirsty raiders which wrought such annual havoc among their cattle and sheep.

Among primitive societies it is customary to refrain from mentioning your enemy by name. The various common euphemisms for Satan are a case in point, and the rule was also applied to wolves. During the dangerous period toward the end of December it was absolutely forbidden both in Prussia and Lithuania to refer to a wolf as such lest it devoured you on the spot. Instead it was known as "Vermin," a title which it would not readily associate with itself, but which would give the user power over it. In Mecklenberg it was generally believed that to mention a wolf by name was, as we say, to talk of the devil, and likely to make one appear. In fact a shepherd would have preferred to apostrophize Satan at this season, if he had had the choice, rather than mention the dreaded wolf. An amusing instance of this taboo is mentioned by Sir James Frazer. A farmer who had a bailiff called "Wolf" dared not use his name during the Christmas season, and referred to him instead as "Mr. Monster." Presumably the bailiff had no objection to the use of this uncomplimentary sobriquet at this season, or possibly the farmer as a point of delicacy avoided employing it to his face.

The same superstition was found in Sweden where peasant girls avoided referring to wolves by name in the confident belief that they would then refrain from attacking the herds. Endearing names for unendearing creatures occur in Hesiod, one of the earliest of Greek poets, like "Bone-less" for octopus and "House-carrier" for snails, and in modern times such titles as "Grey Legs," "Golden Tooth" and "The Silent One" are applied to wolves. In Carpathia the Huzuls call the bear and wolf "Big One" and "Little One" respectively, while the

Eskimos name the wolf "Greycoat." Some of these titles might be hardly supposed to deceive a beast of the cunning and sagacity of the wolf, but then it is a dogma of folklore that evil things are remarkably stupid and easily taken in by the simplest of ruses.

The ancient superstition that a man was struck dumb if a wolf saw him first is referred to by Virgil in a famous passage. The shepherd Moeris laments that in his youth he would often sing the sun to sleep, but now he has forgotten his songs. Indeed his voice itself is leaving him "as if the wolves had seen him first." The elder Pliny also mentions the same belief. "But in Italy too," he says, "it is believed that the sight of a wolf is harmful, and if they see a man before he sees them he is temporarily struck dumb." This, as we have seen, is certainly the experience of people in France who were rendered speechless with terror by a wolf's sudden appearance. It is not indeed so much a superstition as a fact, as it is difficult to imagine in Europe any experience more terrifying than to be unexpectedly confronted by a wolf. The same Moeris was also credited by Virgil with the power of turning himself into a wolf through the agency of drugs. "These herbs and poisons," the shepherd Daphnis says, "plucked in Pontus, Moeris himself gave me as a gift. Helped by these I have often seen Moeris change into a wolf, summon up the dead from the depths of the grave, and move the standing corn into other men's fields."

That men could project their souls by turning themselves into wild beasts is still widely believed. In central Asia shamans while in trance claim to be able to travel great distances, and in Latvia and the Balkans and even in Ireland they are commonly supposed to do so in animal form. Now the wolf is among the strongest and most widely travelled of beasts, and so when selecting a suitable form in which to wander it represented an obvious choice. In other regions like India and South America adepts identified themselves with tigers or jaguars, while in countries where wolves were unknown witches were believed to roam in the shape of cats or hares. Nevertheless wherever the wolf was common it was usually preferred. For some curious reason there always existed a curious intimacy between men and their chief enemy. It was probably, from a psychological point of view, a love-hate relationship based on fear and mutual respect, but whatever its origin it undoubtedly existed. The realization too that wolves could be domesticated over a period and converted by judicious crossing into faithful watch-dogs probably had something to do with it, and this led men to regard them, despite their savagery, as something in the nature of potential friends. At any rate, magical relationship with the wolf was sought whether through the medium of totem or the black arts.

There was also, of course, the extraordinary belief that children were sometimes mothered by she-wolves. The most familiar form of the legend is found in the story of Romulus and Remus. This famous pair were the twin sons of the Vestal virgin Rhea Silvia who had been raped by the god Mars and imprisoned as a punishment for having broken her vow of chastity. Meanwhile the two helpless babes were thrown into the Tiber, as it was quite usual to get rid of illegitimate children either by exposure or some other means. However they were washed ashore near where a she-wolf was slaking her thirst. Attracted by their cries the beast approached them, but instead of killing and eating them she was mastered by mother-love. She offered the hungry infants her teats to suck until their hunger was sated, and then either carried them up to a cave on the Palatine hill or was disturbed by the approach of a shepherd. The shepherd who was called Faustulus reared the two children as his own sons, and finally they were acknowledged by their grandfather Numitor.

Now the legend may and has been scouted on more than one ground, but the problem of the wolf remains. Even today a captive wolf in a cave near the Tarpeian Rock at Rome reminds visitors of the story, and the famous bronze statue of the she-wolf on the Capitol dates from the sixth century B.C. The question of interest is whether wolves do in fact, under certain circumstances suckle human infants, and the answer must be emphatically yes. The she-wolf, as has been frequently remarked, is a most faithful dam, and quite willing to sacrifice her life in the defence of her offspring. So when deprived of them she is temporarily inconsolable, and perfectly willing to accept substitutes to relieve the pain in her breasts. Human children are in the nature of things not easy to come by, but in countries where exposure is practised wolves must from time to time have lighted on living infants and, if the wolves chanced to be deprived females, have offered them milk. Some years ago an Indian hunter followed a she-wolf to her den, and was astonished to find that her litter included two small children as well as her own cubs. The children ran about on all fours howling and snarling like their foster brethren, and bit and growled angrily when the hunter attempted to handle them. They were in due course rescued, but proved to be hopeless imbeciles incapable of being reared as human beings. Other cases have been recorded, although it has not always been established that the foster-mother was in fact a wolf. However it seems pretty evident that although children are able to survive and even thrive on a diet of wolf's milk, if they are left for any time they develop wolf-like characteristics and remain in a state of arrested development for the rest of their lives. Romulus and Remus were saved in time, but the Indian children were not so fortunate. Of course, even supposing that a she-wolf happens to take a fancy to a human baby the chances of its survival in company with her own fierce offspring and even fiercer mate are, to say the least, extremely slender. So more cases of wolves suckling infants may have occurred than have been recorded as the babes most usually died in the process.

Wolf-madness in which the victim imagines that he has become endowed with the characteristics of a wolf, or that he has actually changed into one, is a form of mania known to medical science, and many of the confessions of so-called werewolves in medieval times must be explained in this way. One wretch who had been imprisoned while suffering from this delusion explained to a visitor that he was really free.

At night, he said, the heavy shackles which bound him were loosened, and he fled in wolf form through the open window. He claimed furthermore that this power of transformation had been bestowed upon him by the Devil one Easter, and that ever since he had been a werewolf.

Such examples of lunacy must have been familiar in ancient days, and probably some of the novices in totem ceremonies were already half-crazed. Blood-lust, at any rate, was a well-known phenomenon and victims so affected often behaved like rabid wolves. The grim berserkers of Norse legend undoubtedly had their counterparts in fact, men who were outlawed from the community because of their murderous tendencies, and forced to seek a living like Lycaon in the wild. Greek heroes too could go berserk through brooding on some real or imagined slight. Achilles in the *Iliad* is a case in point, for when he finally decides to go to war he behaves like a rampaging wolf. His followers are likened to wolves in a famous passage as he marshalls them to fight.

> They were like ravening wolves in all their unspeakable fury, which have brought down a great antlered stag in the mountains and are tearing it to pieces. Then away the pack goes to lap the surface of the black water from some dark spring with their thin tongues, belching gouts of flesh. And their hearts are fearless in their breasts for all that their bellies are swollen.

Ajax too went berserk after Achilles' death when he failed to be awarded the hero's armour, and in his madness attacked the cattle, just as if he had been a wolf. But such outrages were by no means confined to heroes, for cases of cattle-maiming by rustics still occur today and often when the moon is full. This latter feature is of course associated with lunatics by derivation, and it is interesting to note that the soldier in Petronius' werewolf story suffered transformation under a moon. The connection between lunatics and the moon has not been established, though the effect of the shining satellite is not in doubt. Dogs and wolves too behave strangely at such times, howling in concert as if demented or entranced.

In modern Greece the belief that certain persons are what are termed *kallikantzari* is firmly believed. They too are supposed to suffer from periodic attacks of blood frenzy, during which they indulge in murder and rape. Children born between Christmas and Twelfth Night are congenitally disposed to such bouts of madness, and are also credited with cannibalistic tendencies. In Macedonia they are actually called "wolves," and as much care is deemed requisite to prevent their attacks as when dealing with vampires. When *kallikantzari* are on the prowl all houses are sealed with pitch or garlic, or bound with magic straw ropes.

In Naples men born on Christmas Day are still believed to be werewolves, and to be able to run about on all fours. They are also believed to possess long tails, and although they retain their human form to behave in other respects like wolves.

The ability to run on all fours was noted by authorities investigating cases of supposed lycanthropy during the seventeenth century in France. A youth of fourteen called Jean Grenier alleged before the ecclesiastical court of Roche-Chalans that he was in fact a werewolf as a result of a demoniacal gift, and that he had killed and eaten children. He also accused his father of being a werewolf and possessing a wolfskin and another man of having a skin and a supply of magic ointment. Fortunately not even the church authorities were deceived by these vainglorious claims, and the boy was pronounced mad and confined in a convent. There he behaved like a wolf, running on all fours with ease and eating in a manner that was more animal than human. The origin of such manifestations of insanity are hard to divine, though the conditions of living coupled with the universal belief in witchcraft and magic were undoubtedly contributory causes. It was, indeed, even supposed that some abject wretches were driven by hunger and neglect to indulge in beast-like activities, though it is difficult to be certain after such a long interval. It was, of course, only on rare occasions that the authorities were prepared to grant the accused the benefit of the doubt and absolve them from devilish practices. Indeed one Inquisitor boasted proudly that he had put to death more than six hundred werewolves during the latter years of the sixteenth century and the beginning of the seventeenth! How many of these poor creatures were victims of their own delusions, or arrested on false charges will never be known. Some were probably apprehended merely on their appearance, for according to one authority those who were afflicted by the wolfish or canine madness could be recognized by their pale faces, tearless eyes, dry tongue and burning thirst. They were supposed to roam abroad during the month of February imitating wolves and dogs. Doubtless many of them were suffering from what medical authorities describe as degradation of the personality, and really believed that they had become beasts. Nebuchadnezzar appears to have been similarly afflicted, for he is described in the Bible as living like a wild animal, while "his hairs were grown like eagles' feathers, and his nails like birds' claws."

Yet when all is said and done the mystery of the strange intimacy between man and wolf remains. It is perhaps best typified by an Eskimo story recorded by Helge Instad in *Nunamiut*. The wolf plays an important part in most Eskimo tales, as is only to be expected in the case of so cunning and impressive a beast. But the curious fact is that the Eskimo mind tends to attribute to the wolf a human brain and feelings, and regards it as thinking like a man. Also it is supposed to possess an immortal soul, so that it may never be destroyed in the fullest sense, but can take vengeance on its slayers. Indeed the Eskimos are always at great pains to perform certain religious rites when they kill a wolf in order not to offend it. According to one tale a wolf called Magûla plans to avenge his sister who had been killed by the hunters, and sets out to do so in company with his brother. When they arrive at the hunter's hut they recognized him by a tattoo mark over his eye, but as they have no knife they cannot kill him. This seems very strange since they are fierce wolves, but the Eskimo story-teller regards everything from his own point of view. However, the wolves hear that knives are obtainable from another tribe, and set out once more to obtain one. On the way Magûla gets caught in a trap, and the hunter flays him and cuts off his head. Now comes the interesting part of the legend. Magûla is reported as feeling no pain, and as being fully conscious of what is going forward. Meanwhile the hunter returns home with the skin and carcase, but has to make a wide detour in order to avoid the trail of a menstruating woman. When he arrives he follows a curious ritual. He first walks round his tent, stamps hard five times, and shouts at the top of his voice. Everyone then realizes that he has killed a wolf. Magûla's skin is hung up, and we learn what he is thinking as the hunter carefully washes and changes his clothes. A feast follows, but the Eskimo does not neglect to put out some meat to feed Magûla's soul. Great care is also exercised to ensure that the cooking-pot is not allowed to boil over, and that no one touches the hunter's cooking utensils. He is also denied fat or gravy, and before the party retire they hang up their valuables and invite Magûla to take what he likes. He is obliged to wait five days, and then chooses two flint knives as well as two forehead straps set with crystal beads. One set is for his brother, who has apparently throughout the proceedings been waiting to join him, and with their aid the two wolves succeed in taking the murderer's life and so in avenging their sister. They then return to report to their parents just as human beings might do.

Finally mention must be made of the superstition that some people possessed the power of leading wolves. Witches, as has been seen, were popularly believed to be able to change human beings into wolves, and to keep them, like Circe, in the vicinity of their dwellings. But the power to lead wolves was something different. It meant that when a pack appeared in a given neighbourhood it was sometimes thought to have been brought there by human agency. An eye-witness in France, during the nineteenth century, described how one night, when the moon was full, a prerequisite always for witchcraft and the black arts, he had seen a man seated in a glade with a pack of wolves gambolling around him. Probably they were dogs, but whatever the truth of the story, the belief has survived in backward areas right down to the present day. Colour was lent to it by the custom of itinerant beggars roaming the countryside accompanied by tame bears or wolves. During 1879 one of these vagabonds appeared leading a muzzled and starved-looking wolf which he threatened would attack and devour the local villagers unless they gave him bread. Hunters, however, remained firmly unsuperstitious, and it was mainly due to their courage and pertinacity that wolves were exterminated in regions where they had formerly been common.

*Chapter Fourteen*

# The Hunter Hunted

THE treasures of Florence's Palazzo Vecchio are world famous, but among the gigantic frescoes, painted masterpieces and gilded ceilings one object takes the eye. It is an enormous tapestry in grand point depicting a pack of near life-sized wolves assembled round a gin. From the latter one of their number dangles like a robber from a gibbet, while the others regard him in silent misery. For some inexplicable reason the whole work is deeply disturbing, and after gazing at it for any length of time one begins to share the great beasts' sorrow for the fate which has overtaken their fellow-creature. Moreover, one finds oneself feeling and thinking like a wolf and becoming conscious of an atavistic yearning for the wild. The artist again has succeeded in endowing the wolves with individual personalities, and one begins to mourn with them as men mourn for a brother in the knowledge that they too are mortal and soon must die. Clearly the design was intended to evoke such feelings, though the man who set the gin-trap had far different ideas.

From the remote days when man first evolved upon the earth the wolf has been his constant enemy. In the earliest times he must have constituted an easy prey for the gigantic prehistoric wolves which roamed in great packs across Europe and Asia, for apart from the ability to take refuge in a cave or tree he was virtually defenceless against their assaults. One advantage, however, he did possess, and that was the power to think. So he dug deep pits around his dwelling places, set sharp stakes in the bottom and covered them with twigs. Pits are the simplest form of wolf-trap and are still largely employed in the Balkans and elsewhere. But wolves are cunning, suspicious creatures so the pits have to be carefully camouflaged and this can lead to human tragedies too. The occasion when a fiddler returning from a wedding had the misfortune to stumble into a pit which already contained a live wolf has already been mentioned, and history duly repeated itself during the severe weather of February 1963.

Wolves have always been a pest in Yugoslavia, and strenuous efforts have been made to trap them or kill them in various ways. As the well-tried method of digging pits usually proved efficacious many were sunk near wolf-runs in the forests and carefully covered with sticks and snow. Pieces of offal and meat were then laid on the surface, or a goat was tethered near to the brink. During the recent winter the inhabitants of Rogozin in Serbia were often roused at night by the howl of wolves, and pits were dug in the neighbouring woods to protect the village. In order to be effective the camouflage had to be perfect, and not everyone was aware of their precise location. One night a man called Miladi Stojkovic was returning home when he fell into a pit over ten feet deep. This was bad enough in all conscience, for the pit was so constructed that it was impossible to climb out until help arrived. Besides, it was bitterly cold, and it would have been easy enough to freeze to death before morning. Just then a fetid odour attracted the man's attention, and to his horror he observed two eyes gleaming balefully from the opposite corner. The realization that he shared his prison with a wolf all but drove him frantic, but his cries for help were muffled and unheard. The wretched man's state of mind may well be appreciated. Any moment the beast might leap at him, and in the event of a struggle he had nothing with which to defend himself, not even a knife. Well aware that to fall asleep might easily prove fatal he crouched shivering in the darkness, while his grim companion did the same. All night long man and his oldest enemy watched one another narrowly and waited, and when dawn came Stojkovic was half crazy with strain and fear. Soon the man who had set the trap arrived from the village to see what he had caught, and was astonished to find a human victim. After shooting the wolf he helped Stojkovic from the pit, but was shocked to note that the dreadful experience had turned his hair grey.

Pits were widely used in France during the nineteenth century, and were normally sited in clearings in the forests or alongside buildings or walls. They were twelve feet deep and the bait was a live duck which would attract the wolves with its quacking. A shovel was then laid across the opening with holes drilled in the handle for the insertion of thin sticks. The whole was then covered with a layer of straw and treated with wolf-dung if the latter was available.

The captured beast was raised from its confinement by means of a clasp fastened to a pole, and when helpless in mid-air it was a simple matter to tie its paws together with running nooses. Once out, its head was pinned to the ground with a fork while its lips were sewn up with shoe-makers' thread to muzzle its terrible jaws. After being flayed alive the wolves' carcases were cooked in huge cauldrons with milk, cheese and wheat, and finally the skins were stuffed in order to train the dogs to attack them.

Such methods may seem cruel, but the wolf itself is a cruel beast and could scarcely expect to be treated better. By using pits M. Naffrichoux, a schoolmaster from Callefrouin at the end of the last century, was responsible for the destruction of many wolves and cubs near the castle of Bel-Air in the great forest of Charente.

It was also the custom in France to ambush wolves by putting out a dead animal as bait and waiting for the beasts to arrive. The profession of wolf-stalker was naturally a dangerous one, and the more so since those who practised it usually preferred to work alone. However, a wounded wolf was another matter, and before venturing in pursuit the wise stalker went in search of local aid. At one time a she-wolf caused widespread devastation and panic throughout the communes of Dougat, Echellat and Hiersac in Charente, and it was left to a keeper of seventy-five to track the beast down. The task was no easy one as the month was May when there was plenty of cover, and no snow to show footprints. Also, the entire area was thickly forested and the location of the wolf was a difficult task. However the keeper was not one to give in easily once he had set his mind to a task, and after setting baits in various likely places he subsequently visited each one in turn. He timed his visits for dawn and dusk when the wolf was most likely to feed, and in due course surprised it very early one morning. At first he could see nothing, though he could hear the bones crackling as the wolf ate the meat, and then he saw the "candles" shining through the mist. Aiming carefully at where the heart should be, he slowly pressed the trigger. But instead of dropping dead the great beast ran off howling into the forest. The hardy hunter crossed himself. Perhaps after all the villagers were right, and the beast was in fact a *loup-garou*. On the other hand none but a fool would attempt to follow a wounded wolf alone into a thick forest. So he came out for help, and had the good fortune to fall in with two women guarding their sheep. When he asked them to accompany him they naturally demurred, but when assured that the wolf was mortally wounded they reluctantly gave in. Returning, the keeper soon found the blood-trail leading from the bait, and following it he and his two companions eventually arrived in the centre of the wood. A sudden movement ahead then attracted their attention, and they found, to their relief, the wolf dying under a tree.

The courage required for such an excursion by an aged man and two unarmed women was naturally considerable, for a wounded wolf could prove a terrible foe and there was always the danger of rabies. But in regions where wolves were common men and women alike were prepared to risk their lives in order to protect those of others. Peasants rarely ventured abroad unless armed with pikes or pistols, and sometimes whole batteries of muskets were trained on a dead beast with threads attached from it to the triggers. Woe betide any unsuspecting person who chanced to pass that way, for to disturb the bait or touch the strings was to invite a deadly broadside.

Sometimes nets were woven out of thin cord and spread across the runs, while bands of villagers drove the wolves before them blowing trumpets and making a din. But this method was apt to prove less effective than guns or pits as the wolves had a habit of breaking through the nets or cunningly avoiding them at the last moment.

One of the most successful ways of destroying wolves was, of course, by the use of poison, though its indiscriminate employment naturally imperilled the lives of dogs and other creatures too. But where wolves were concerned no holds were barred. In France aconite proved most effective if used in the following fashion. A pound of nux vomica was mixed with sops or other suitable food and used to poison some unwanted dog. Twelve bulbs of aconite were then procured, and after being pounded in a mortar were mixed with the remainder of the powdered nux vomica together with a handful of horse-hair. The dead dog's legs were tied together for ease of transportation, and the poison inserted by making holes in the flesh. The carcase was then carried on a pole to a dung heap and left to rot for a period of days, before being removed to a place frequented by wolves. The latter were in due course attracted by the dog's scent, and would feed on it perhaps for as many as three days together. All such as did so were doomed to die a lingering death often far from the bait. When it was desired to recover the pelts it was customary to treat the corpse of the dog in addition with corrosive sublimate. This poison was of deadly efficacy, and correspondingly difficult to obtain, but it was guaranteed to kill a wolf in a very short time and usually within close proximity of the bait.

Poison proved fatal at most times to wolves, and was perhaps the most telling single factor in their ultimate disappearance from regions where they had been formerly common. It was particularly effective in winter, when snow destroyed any tell-tale human scent, and the wolves were anyhow too hungry to bother. Dogs were chosen as bait because they were commonly regarded as the wolf's favourite food, and as likely to prove eminently attractive to a species addicted to cannibalism.

Although dogs not used as bait were provided with spiked collars to protect them from the attacks of wolves, it is ironical to note that one was killed and eaten near Saint-Preuil in Charente, all except for its neck and head! The armament, of course, tends to be less effective in the case of some smaller breeds, but in Turkey, according to Mr. Ian Tully, where big dogs are the rule the collar is said to prove an effective deterrent. Certainly the spikes are sharp and strong enough to puncture tyres as tourists soon learn to their cost!

In Russia poison is used on a commercial scale to capture wolves for their pelts. As the latter are at their best in winter the baits are only laid in hard weather when the snow lies deep on the ground. They are scattered over a wide area through the forests and, as at that season wolves tend to pack, large numbers of beasts succumb. Collection is simple as a round of the baits is made by a train of sledges drawn by a caterpillar tractor, and the wolf-prints are easy to follow in the snow. So powerful is the drug employed that the wolves collapse within a few yards of the bait and extensive searches are unnecessary. Many are still alive when found, but instead of snapping furiously they usually lie supine. Indeed a drugged wolf permits itself to be handled with impunity in a way that other carnivora would not. Capture in any form seems to break its spirit, so that people like the unfortunate Stojkovic were safer than they knew. Whole packs of drugged wolves are then piled like sheep on trailers, and driven to a centre to be flayed. Indeed the success of this method must cause concern among such as are unwilling that the wolf should become an extinct species.

In France the destruction of wolves has always been formally organized on a regional basis by la Louveterie. From the time of Charlemagne grand *louvetiers* or wolf-hunters were appointed, and their deputies held office in every canton. Their function was to rid their neighbourhood of wolves by any means at their disposal, and all other state officials were required by law to assist them. During the sixteenth century Charles IX had considered it sufficient to warn his subjects to expel by means of shouts and stones all the "red and black" beasts to be found in their area. They were, however, strangely charged not to harm them in the process presumably because wolves were preserved for hunting. Nevertheless subsequent edicts soon outlawed the wolf, and battues were organized in every district. It was not until the reign of Henry IV (1553-1610) that a royal pack of wolf-hounds was formed, but royal hunts became the fashion under Francis I (1494-1547), and the cry *"Harloup!"* was often heard in the forests of Charente. As hunts continued for several days it was customary for the king and his retinue to put up for the night in the various châteaux, and it was a gallant sight to see them all assembled in the morning, the hunters in their brilliant livery, and the ladies mounted on their richly accoutred mares.

In the time of Louis XIV the Dauphin was nominally in charge of wolf-hunting, but the jealousy that existed between the lieutenants and the officials responsible for the forests and fisheries acted as a brake on hunting and benefited the wolves. Indeed in 1787 the Corps of Wolf-Hunters was suppressed altogether in the interests of economy, but so great was the devastation caused by wolves during the Revolutionary era that Napoleon revived the office in 1804. Several letters of the time bear eloquent witness to the contemporary state of affairs in La Vendée. As a decree had been passed forbidding civilians to carry arms the wolves increased in numbers. A letter from the sub-prefect at Deux-Sèvres in 1798 reads as follows: "Citizen, I have instigated several successful wolf-hunts, but the five or six beasts accounted for hardly scratch the surface of the problem. The number of wolves has grown so great that complaints are reaching me from every district. Not a night goes by but oxen, cows, calves and sheep are slaughtered in every commune."

A second letter from a commissioner called Bisson reads: "It has come to my knowledge that the wolves are parading in packs six, ten or fifteen strong and are even attacking the shepherds guarding the flocks."

Most *lieutenants de louveterie* devoted their lives to their calling, and the annals of France are filled with accounts of their exploits. They were reputed never to take a holiday, and so successful were their methods that they left their twentieth-century successors with virtually no problem.

The private hunting of wolves for sport was also widely practised in France throughout the eighteenth and nineteenth centuries. A notable exponent of this art was the eighth Duke de la Rochefoucauld who was so mastered by his love of the chase that even when he was past riding he used to hunt wolves from his carriage. As he sped along sounding his horn all the peasants assembled to watch him pass, and handicapped though he was he was yet responsible for the death of a wolf which had been ravaging the neighbourhood and killed several shepherds.

One of the most famed wolf-hunters in Charente during the eighteenth century was Gaston de Céris, who in his time rid the district of countless wolves. He lived in the Château de la Foye, which was situated in a wild district on the confines of Deux-Sèvres. There he hunted almost every day, and his pack was as well known as John Peel's. It consisted of some thirty white and orange-coloured hounds which he dearly loved and which were thoroughly experienced in the pursuit of wolves. Gaston was a jockey-sized cavalier, but possessed of the courage of twenty lions. Everyone loved him, and during the Terror he lived on a farm disguised as a peasant, safe in the knowledge that none of his dependants would ever give him away. He died in 1804 while out hunting after suffering a fall from his horse.

Another famous hunter of the time was Monsieur de Montemboeuf, who lived in a manor above the town of that name, and hunted a royal pack. His hounds were a present from Louis XV, and were white touched with orange, and had square heads, short hair and long limbs—perhaps not unlike modern fox-hounds. Their sense of hearing was said to be exceedingly acute, and their staying powers were remarkable. Once on a wolf's scent they never paused or faltered until they had brought the beast to bay. Unfortunately their master's qualities were not appreciated by the Revolutionaries, and he was guillotined in 1793.

The Sire de Bois-Coûteau who was born in 1740 devoted his entire life and resources to hunting. Having no interest in cultivation, he permitted his estates round Fleurignac to deteriorate, while he purged the entire area of wolves. His father had left him a considerable fortune, but soon there was scarcely enough left to support the small pack of twelve big white and yellow hounds whose pluck and endurance were only matched by those of Montemboeuf himself. Their master sacrificed his all for them, dressed in home-spun, and deprived himself of everything but absolute necessities. By the end of his life all that remained of the family treasures were a silver-plated musket engraved with his coat of arms, a hunter's knife with a silver hilt and a whip with an ivory whistle. Nothing could stop him when out hunting, and in his anxiety to bring the largest wolves to bay he would eagerly scour the countryside on his tough little pony. If he failed to run the beast down by nightfall, he would put up at a neighbouring house or inn, and continue the chase on the morrow. Often an old wolf would run for three days on end before standing to face the hounds. Whenever this happened Bois-Coûteau would dismount and despatch the beast with a knife thrust. Then came the triumphant journey home of a hundred miles or more.

One day he found a big wolf not far from Angoulême. The beast proved worthy of its age and stature and ran for three whole days. On the evening of the third the hunt arrived at the mouth of the Gironde. There the wolf took to water, and before Bois-Coûteau could prevent them the hounds were all swimming for dear life.

Despite his anguished shouts and entreaties they continued in pursuit of the wolf which was attempting to reach the further shore many miles distant. Whether it succeeded or failed he never knew for he saw neither it nor his hounds again. His grief was so pitiful after this disaster that some local hunters were moved to present him with the nucleus of a fresh pack. With these he achieved some notable feats, and his end at an advanced age was probably the one he would have chosen. He died on the hunting field, disembowelled by a lone wolf which he was trying to knife.

A certain Monsieur Victor Roux de Reilhac married Monsieur Montemboeuf's daughter, and became a lifelong friend of another noted wolf-hunter, Monsieur de la Besge. The latter owned the Château de la Boulonnie in Vienne, and the pair decided to join forces in order to hunt out old wolves by relays. De Reilhac was a remarkable hunter, and his pack rarely failed to bring to bay any wolf it had scented. He was always accompanied by a huntsman known as Old Peter, who shared all his activities, hopes and disappointments and was treated less as a servant than as a valued friend. On hunting days men and beasts were expected to be ready by three in the morning, and there were no breaks for food until six at night. On one occasion he and his friend La Besge scoured the forest of La Braconne for more than three hours before they finally succeeded in unharbouring a wolf. The beast then ran for sixteen hours before it was finally brought to bay in the vicinity of Limoges. In his time the hunter was credited with having destroyed more than a thousand young wolves. These, once their lair was discovered, were brought to bay in turn and despatched by a shrewd blow from a stick on the back of the neck. This remarkable hunter lived to be ninety-two, and wore a wolf on his buttons and the legend "Where to flee?" He fulfilled for many years the office of *lieutenant de louveterie* in the district of Angoulême, founded the Société de la Braconne, and filled the forest with stags and hinds imported from Rambouillet. In character he was gay, affable, witty and generous. A hunting fanfare was dedicated to him, and the older inhabitants could never revive his memory without emotion.

A she-wolf's willingness to sacrifice herself for her cubs, though more than half-grown and already hunting for themselves, is well illustrated by an account of a hunt near Limoges in 1853. The presence of *louvarts* in the district had been brought to the notice of the *lieutenant de louveterie*, and on the morning of 13th August the hounds followed the tracks of one of them. Its dam was roused by the noise of the hunt, and leaving her lair deliberately attempted to draw the hounds off the scent. She led them on a wide détour, but the hunter realized her intention and headed the pack off in the original direction. As a result of this manœuvre the first cub was killed at the end of an hour, and a second and third somewhat later. The she-wolf returned and laid her scent with the aim of leading the hounds away into a wild area, criss-crossed with streams, where tracking would have been difficult if not impossible. The lieutenant, however, still refused to be diverted, and as a result of his pertinacity the two remaining cubs were killed. The she-wolf escaped and everyone agreed that she had proved herself the heroine of the hour.

One notable trapper called Jean Guillot made it his business to destroy wolf-cubs. Like most men of his profession he worked alone, though he sometimes took his son with him in order to teach him the art. Whenever a report reached him that a she-wolf or her cubs had been seen, he would command his informant to show him the spot. Mounting a hillock he would then politely inquire where the man supposed the den to be. The latter would then quickly scan the adjoining woods and indicate some likely looking feature. Whereupon Guillot would smile.

"D'you really think so?" he would rejoin. "Then I fear you're mistaken. If there are any wolves about they'll be down there." And he'd point in a different direction. Nine times out of ten he proved to be right, for his knowledge was based on long experience. On approaching the spot which he had indicated he would order his companion or companions to remain where they were while he entered the den single-handed. To defend himself he carried a stick and a basket for the cubs' reception. After a period which varied according to the difficulty of the operation he would emerge in triumph with the basket full of cubs. Curiously enough the dams never attacked him, though they frequently followed him through the forest, at a respectful distance. One day he arrived at the house where young Raymond Rollinat, who in later life became the leading authority on the wolves of France, lived with his two aunts, and offered the cubs for sale. But one of the aunts proved adamant.

"Buy yourself a bear-cub if it will give you any pleasure," she exploded, "or even a lion-cub, but I won't have a wolf in my home!"

In order to encourage the local peasants to exterminate the wolves in their own districts rewards were offered which increased in value as the beasts became progressively rarer. During the Napoleonic era forty francs was the official payment for a wolf in France, sixty for a she-wolf in cub, twenty for a cub itself and 150 for a rabid beast or one that had attacked a human being. Rewards were paid right down to the end of the nineteenth century and Mr. S. H. Moore, who had lived in the Massif Central as a boy, describes how, coming down the village street early one November, he noticed a small crowd in front of the Mairie.

> There was seldom anything in that tiny bourg to draw one away from a big logwood fire and the glorious books of old France, so I asked an acquaintance what was going on. His only answer was to point to a barrow near the Mairie steps on which lay stretched out the finest wolf I had ever seen. The man who had wheeled it in was perspiring profusely and telling his story—how he had seen something nosing round the barn, had got his gun, and shot the beast point-blank: "Te! La! Da'm mazeau" (Right in the muzzle); how he was now waiting for the fixed reward of 100 francs; how he wished it had been a *louve* (she-wolf) that he might have got 150 . . . still, as it was a fine one, there was always the pelt!

Perhaps the most sporting method of taking wolves is to course them like hares. The practice was formerly common in Russia where Borzois were employed to run wolves down and hold them until the hunters came up on horseback to despatch them on the spot. Foxhounds were used to find the wolves and the Borzois were slipped at them when they broke from cover. Though the wolf is a tireless runner over a long distance it becomes quickly winded in a short chase so that the courses were rarely of long duration. Borzois, being lighter, were considerably faster than their savage quarry, but very few had the pluck to tackle a wolf alone. In Scotland deerhounds were employed in a similar manner, as we know from the anecdote already recorded when Mary Queen of Scots once ordered while out hunting the strongest and swiftest hound to be slipped at a wolf. In Ireland wolf-hounds were used precisely like Borzois in Russia, but the tactics employed there have already been described. That a dog should be able to run down its much heavier and fiercer cousin is somewhat remarkable. But then wolves are essentially cowards at heart, whereas a dog, being domesticated and with a master to back it, enjoys a considerable moral advantage. Usually, too, a wolf was already badly frightened by the time it was called upon to expend its reserves in a course.

The problem of the supposed basic relationship between dogs and wolves has never been satisfactorily resolved. Broadly speaking authorities are divided into two schools: viz., those who believe that all dogs are originally descended from wolves, and those who maintain that the domestic beast's ancestor was quite distinct, in fact a wild dog. The circumstance that wolves will cross with dogs, and that certain species like Alsatian sheep-dogs and the various Eskimo breeds, closely resemble wolves and are indeed sometimes deliberately crossed with them in order to improve the strain is strongly in favour of the former view. On the other hand all recorded attempts to tame wolves have ultimately failed.

During the last century the Conte de Saint-Aulaire reared a young wolf in his château and trained it to accompany him whenever he visited his forests and estates. The animal learned to follow his horse like a dog, but one day when his horse nearly threw him while leaping a ditch his cloak fell to the ground. The wolf seized it in a flash and began to tear it to pieces, and resisted every effort to persuade it to release its hold. Only then did the count realize what his fate would have been had he been inside the cloak!

A similar anecdote is told about another French gentleman, Monsieur de Lafoud of Combiers, who had also tamed a wolf. While out riding one day with one of his friends the latter prognosticated that sooner or later the beast would cost him dear. To prove his point he let his cape fall, and at once the wolf seized it and tore it to pieces. Its master was so shaken by this savage performance that he immediately killed his pet.

Indeed, experience leads to the conclusion that although you could keep a wolf as a pet until it was two years old, it was certain sooner or later to betray its treacherous character. A butcher who kept a pair of wolves in captivity before the First World War was horrified to discover one morning that his pets had killed all his sheep.

The modern way of hunting wolves in Poland is on foot with guns and has been described in fascinating detail by Mr. Puchalski, the famous naturalist, in *The Field*. The first step is to locate the area in which the pack is operating. Their presence may be indicated by their howls in the autumn when they are mating, but they are hard to track before the first falls of snow. Once their resting place has been discovered word is sent round to the neighbouring villages inviting volunteers to come and assist. Long ropes festooned with rags are then piled on sleighs and carried to the point where the tracks lead into the forest, but do not emerge again. This may well involve a journey of upwards of thirty kilometres as wolves are great travellers, and often hunt far from their lairs. Two sleighs are then despatched in opposite directions to cordon off the area by suspending the ropes on trees and bushes at the height of a wolf's head. The use of ropes might appear at first to be a laughably inadequate method of keeping wolves confined in a particular area, yet the beast's native suspicion contributes to its own undoing. The rags frighten it, and it takes pains to avoid the rope, suspecting a trap. The area enclosed may extend for several kilometres, with a gap for the wolves to bolt. There the guns are massed. The first shot rouses the wolves from their rest, and meeting the rope they dash for the gap. When the leaders are shot the rest break back and try to find another escape route. Failing they return inevitably to the gap and others meet their doom. Finally in panic they rush the barrier and the remainder make good their escape.

Another method practised in the highland parts of Poland was recently described by Mr. MacGregor-Hastie. Wolves, of course, will follow when famished any scent that is laid for them, so a hunter trailing a dead goat climbs high above the snow-line to attract the wolves from their lairs. If none appear he returns and drags the goat about again quite oblivious of personal danger. The signal that wolves have been seen is sounded on a horn and all the guns massed below are sternly commanded to watch their front. Meantime the hunter descends at a run with a pack of wolves closely following him. The old ones advance in silence, but the young ones make the air reverberate with their excited triple howls. As soon as the wolves are in range the guns start shooting. Still the beasts come on, and only stop at the end of the snow-line where the guns are stationed. Then they slink back up the ridge leaving the dead and dying.

Even more modern methods are now practised in Lapland. Aeroplanes are used to watch for wolves attacking reindeer, and when they are spotted they are shot down from above. Wolves cannot be an easy target for a hunter seated in an aeroplane, yet it is claimed that many are accounted for just the same. The wolf, then, after being harried from land and water is now granted no respite even from the air. In fact everyone's hand is turned against it, and the marvel is that it manages to survive.

*Chapter Fifteen*

# The Wolf Today

DURING the winter of 1962-3 considerable interest was aroused in the Press by reports that wolves had been seen in France, where they were then officially pronounced to be extinct. The most intriguing feature was the locality where the beasts were said to have appeared, for although wolves were once common in the Haute Marne and Côte d'Or none had been seen there for more than a generation. Indeed a man in his nineties was produced to examine the tracks, as he was the last living local inhabitant qualified to do so. But it is impossible to distinguish between the pad-marks of a wolf and those of a large dog, and the tracks found in the snow might have belonged to either.

The evidence, however, was not confined to tracks, for several motorists had reported observing creatures resembling wolves or large dogs roaming in the area. Further reports were received from the Jura and Isère, and finally a hunter in the Vosges claimed to have shot a wolf. Now it is true that well on in the nineteenth century wolves reached France from central Europe, and even penetrated the forest of Fontainebleau. Even so the Paris headline last February claiming that wolves had been seen 124 miles from the capital was greeted with incredulity by competent naturalists. Where, they asked, could the wolves, if wolves they were, have come from? There are now no wolves either in Germany or Switzerland, and so one would have to suppose that they had travelled from Poland. It seemed, however, highly unlikely that they could have succeeded in doing so without being spotted *en route*, and there was still the difficulty of explaining why they should have chosen in the first place to undertake such a long trek to France. That they had come in from Italy or Spain was equally unthinkable as the Haute Marne is far removed from the borders of either country, and they would have certainly been observed in other parts. So the mystery deepened and zoologists waited impatiently for the official report of the beast killed in the Vosges.

The result was bathos. The beast, as many had forecast, proved to have been no wolf at all but a dog gone wild. As it closely resembled the Alaskan breed it was generally assumed that it had originally belonged to an American airman stationed in the area and had been abandoned when the base was evacuated. As for the motorists' reports, these proved just as disappointingly to refer to some alsatians whose owner was to be charged for allowing them to run loose in the area. So the story died though another and possibly more exciting report never reached the British papers.

At the beginning of February a motorist called Monsieur Boruard from La Bussière in Vienne was driving towards Poitiers at about seven in the morning when he saw in his headlights an animal leap up which he immediately identified as a wolf. The beast which had come from the direction of the quarries at Bretigny, two kilometres from Chauvigny on the Route Nationale 151, crossed the road and disappeared in the direction of the village of Pressac. Monsieur Brouard, who was familiar with wolves elsewhere in Europe, immediately reported the occurrence at the local *gendarmerie*, who in turn referred the matter to the master of the hunt. A reconnaissance was made and the local *lieutenant de louveterie* Monsieur Paul Fruchon was advised of what had happened. Footprints were meantime found in the snow at the point which the motorist had indicated and proved on comparison to be far larger than those of any breed of dog living in the area. The tracks led towards Pressac and then doubled back towards the *route nationale*, crossed it again and were then lost near the edge of the Bois Sennebault in the direction of Artiges or du Breuil. As wolves were hunted in Vienne until 1911 no one appears to have regarded the occurrence as particularly out of the ordinary, though few reports about wolves had been received in recent years. Monsieur Brouard's own view was that the beast he had seen was far larger than a dog or even than a wolf-hound, and was neither of the same colour nor shape as the latter. Nevertheless, if the animal was in fact a wolf it seemed odd that one should have appeared in a district where the last reported had been shot as long ago as 1923. This was killed at Queaux by the *lieutenant de louveterie*, Monsieur de la Besge, a descendant of the hunting friend of Monsieur de Reilhac.

The occurrence naturally excited much local curiosity, and it was recalled that during the eighteenth century no fewer than 5,247 wolves had been destroyed in Vienne in the space of fourteen years, and that awards had amounted annually to more than two thousand pounds. Still, it was impossible for a single wolf to survive, so its provenance raised considerable problems. That it should have come all the way from central Europe was even more unlikely than that the supposed wolves of the Haute Marne could have done so. Spain, of course, was a possibility, though even this theory was fraught with difficulties. Wolves, it was true, were capable of covering enormous distances, but it seemed scarcely likely that a single beast could have crossed the Pyrenees, and then made the long journey to Vienne. So the mystery remains, and no one is quite certain whether wolves are extinct in Vienne or not.

A similar mystery surrounds the wolves of Lozère and the wilder regions of the Massif Central. Officially they are extinct there, and have been for many years. Yet certain reliable reports must still raise doubts. During the 1890s wolves were still relatively common throughout the south-western regions, and Mr. Moore has recorded how, as a young man, he and a companion met a she-wolf near Piégut. They were passing through a small copse when "there crossed the road a miserable animal, lean and cadaverous," which though it observed them never ceased in its loping trot and was soon lost to view in the bracken. "It's only a poor bitch of a she-wolf," the Frenchman commented, as though to encounter a wolf was nothing out of the ordinary. But the Englishman was naturally hugely impressed by the first living wolf he had seen out of a zoo.

The winter was a bitter one yet this did not prevent the youth from cycling about the beautiful countryside, and one day he set out for Châlus. It was near here, of course, some years later that the last woman was killed by wolves in France, but none had been reported in the neighbourhood and young Moore's thoughts were far removed from wolves as he gaily pedalled along. Suddenly to his horror he caught sight of an old wolf sitting on a bank ahead calmly awaiting his arrival. "He was a splendid beast, almost as big as my friend in the barrow; unfortunately, however, this fellow's handicap was nil, his *museau* looked, indeed, to be in good working order." As there was no time to dismount the cyclist decided to glide past below him while continuing to gaze straight into his eyes. As he did so the wolf rose slowly from its haunches, and Moore's first reaction was to ride away at top speed. Then he noticed that the road dropped down into a deep forest with no sign of hamlet or habitation. On the other hand he had just passed a farmstead, so he decided to turn back. This, of course, involved passing the wolf again, but appeared in the circumstances to be the lesser of two evils, as he could have been easily ambushed in the forest. He braked hard and swung about to face the wolf once more. Ringing his cycle-bell in an attempt to scare the fearsome creature, he flew past for the second time just as it opened its mouth in a "long-drawn-out coughing yawn." Dismounting at the farm, the boy yelled for a gun as there was a big wolf by the road. But the peasants were suspicious. Who was this stranger with his talk of wolves? The chances were that he was some government busy-body come to catch them out over a licence. By the time they were convinced the youth's request was genuine the wolf had gone, and so had his chance of collecting 100 francs.

During his stay in the Massif Mr. Moore heard many

stories about attacks by wolves, but none more amusing than this. A peasant woman was one day knitting by the roadside watching her beautiful white goat when the animal suddenly gave a peculiar bleat. As she glanced up to see what was the matter a wolf suddenly sprang at the goat which collapsed under its weight. The woman was naturally frightened half out of her wits and was about to run for safety when a prolonged scratching sound and the fall of divots of earth caused her to look back. By a chance in a thousand the goat had lowered its head and wedged the wolf's muzzle between its horns. Try as it would the wolf was unable to free itself, and could do nothing but kick away at the turf and stones. Meanwhile the woman ran for aid to a local farmer who arrived with a knife and slit the wolf from end to end.

But all this was more than sixty years ago, and the question is: do wolves still survive in the Massif Central? Mr. Moore, at any rate, observed one near Les Eyzies on a visit in 1933, and as he was under the impression that they had been long extinct there he made careful inquiries at the nearest village. To his amazement the inhabitants stolidly affirmed that there were no longer any wolves in the district! Clearly their presence was not calculated to boost the tourist trade, yet it seemed scarcely credible that the villagers could have been unaware of their existence.

It is, of course, quite otherwise in Italy, as visitors to Rome are reminded when they visit the supposed site of the Tarpeian Rock. At the bottom is a cave surrounded by an enclosure inhabited by a she-wolf and her mate. Their presence reminds the tourist of the story of Romulus and suggests how closely the city's destiny is linked with wolves. Indeed the beasts still roam the Alban hills and the woods around Tivoli and, although in summer their existence is hardly noticed, during hard winters they sometimes invade Rome itself. In February 1963 considerable alarm was occasioned when it was officially reported that a wolf had been seen skulking in a park in the Villa Borghese district.

Presumably it was busy scavenging, as hyaenas do in the outskirts of Nairobi, and anyway it refrained from attacking any human beings. But this was as nothing to the panic aroused during the grim winter of 1947 when whole packs descended from the surrounding hills and were seen skirting the main roads leading into the city. Fantastic rumours spread. Old women waiting at bus-stops had been killed and eaten, and children done to death on their way to school. And this in modern overcrowded Italy only a few kilometres from Rome!

During the severe winter of 1956 wolves were observed near the main railway line leading inland from Rome to Monte Cassino, and it was then that the unfortunate postman met his fate. Two thousand years before, the poet Horace met a wolf in the same district though he was more fortunate for the beast turned and fled.

> From me a wolf once fled away
> While I was singing Lalage,
> Such monster Daunia home of spears
> Nor Juba, nurse of lions, rears.

During the winter of 1963 packs were reported killing sheep in the heel of Italy, though how long they will survive the big recent industrial revolution in the area is anybody's guess. The extraordinary thing, of course, is that they manage to survive at all in a land where everyone is an amateur sportsman and everything is shot from cats to swallows. Presumably the ordinary hunter avoids the grim and forbidding forests of the Apennines where wolves and wild boars survive in considerable numbers and, it is even rumoured, bears.

Whether the indigenous wolves of Italy are reinforced from time to time by invasions from the Balkans has never been proved. The local stock at any rate never seems to attain epidemic proportions. This is probably due to the same law of nature which appears to control birds of prey. Carnivora, whether bird or beast, require *lebensraum*, and any given tract of land will only support a certain number.

Either the overflow migrates or the parents stop breeding, but the result is the same in either case.

Sixty years ago, according to Norman Douglas, wolves were common in the peninsula of Sorrento. During winter they came down from their lairs on Mount San'Angelo and sometimes attacked human beings. A boy of fifteen was killed and eaten in 1906, all save his feet which were protected by thick boots. A woman, too, was bitten while engaged in cooking macaroni. But such events were comparatively rare. It was otherwise with the dogs, of which more than a hundred were eaten in a single district.

The wolves terrorized the entire neighbourhood right down to the tip of the peninsula, and invaded a cave where goats were harboured in large numbers. The result was a massacre. There have been no references to the depredations of wolves in this part of Italy during recent years, but as it is still a wild area there seems good reason to suppose that wolves still exist there only a few sea-miles from Capri.

Werewolves too were well known in this part of Italy under the name of *lupomanari*. Some were psychopathic cases like the old peasant who lived in a cottage near Sant' Agata and at times of full moon ran about howling and behaving like a wolf.

In Yugoslavia and Rumania wolves still constitute a major pest despite government attempts at extermination. Every year women, children and old men are killed and eaten much as in France during the last century. The sheer number of beasts involved must be very considerable for even when Tito announced the launching of a national campaign it was found impracticable to bring them under control. Curiously enough, despite their evident ubiquity, there have been few references to wolves in accounts of the heroic struggles of the Partisans against the Nazi forces. The same is true of Italy. But then wolves, like other wild animals, are easily frightened by the noise of gunfire, and either lie low or move out of the theatre of operations altogether. This is reported to have happened during World War I when wolves which appeared in the Vosges, Marne and elsewhere in France were thought to have been scared out of districts further east. But much is based on surmise, for so expert are wolves at disguising their activities that they may be easily overlooked even in places where they are common.

When a British archaeologist visited Yugoslavia, Bulgaria and Rumania four years after the end of the Second World War he was advised to keep his windows barred and shuttered at night. Being a fresh-air fiend he naturally demurred until he was informed that the precaution had been found necessary in the district in which he was travelling in order to keep out marauding wolves! Here the packs are certainly reinforced by invasions from Russia and Poland, so that attempts to destroy the native wolf population can only in the nature of things prove partially successful.

The absence of wolves in modern Greece is quite extraordinary. At first sight one might expect the country to be overrun. Yet this is far from the case. There are, of course, wolves on the Albanian and Yugoslavian borders and lone beasts occasionally wander south at all seasons of the year and are duly reported in the Press. The late Professor R. M. Dawkins, who was director of the British School of Archaeology at Athens before the First World War, reported having once seen a dead wolf which had been killed by some villagers and was tremendously impressed by the beast's great size. In July 1949, during the Civil War, a rabid wolf attacked a peasant in the fields near Kozani, bit him severely in the neck and head, and then turned on a woman nursing a baby. After mauling the infant the wolf made off, but was shot by some soldiers during the same afternoon. The unfortunate victims received medical attention. Whether or not they developed rabies was not disclosed, though in the circumstances it seems highly likely.

Wolves again occasionally occur in the Parnassus massif above Delphi as they did in ancient times. But as there is a direct route through the Pindus mountains right into the Balkans it seems curious that more have not been reported. One was seen and shot near the village of Hagios Nikolaos in the Valley of the Muses during the war, but no more were reported despite the near famine conditions for men and beasts alike. Everywhere where inquiries were made the peasants solemnly shook their heads. "No wolves hereabouts, though I did once hear my father say. . . ." Anyhow it would be a bold wolf that braved the sheep-dogs of Helicon which are every bit as big and heavy as a wolf itself.

Probably they have gone from Greece with the forests which are less extensive than they used to be. And the population has increased enormously since the abortive Turkish war. Greeks, too, are keen hunters and it seems highly unlikely that they would ever permit a wolf to survive. Even so, bears are still reputed to exist in the higher ranges of the north-west, so one cannot help wondering why not wolves? Island conditions are certainly no guarantee of their absence as is proved by their presence in Sicily. Wherever the standard of living is low enough and backed by local apathy the wolf, if indigenous, is likely to survive; or again where the country is so extensive that systematic destruction is rarely applied. Such is the case in Spain where wolves are an interesting survival among the local fauna.

Spanish wolves are said on the whole to be smaller than their eastern counterparts and to be neither so destructive nor vicious. They are also said to possess white tipped tails unlike the majority of wolves. Yet even in Spain during hard winters wolves can constitute a menace just as anywhere else. During the winter of 1960 the packs were out in the province of Avila north-west of Madrid, and considerable damage was done to herds of cattle and sheep. The following year the beasts, emboldened by hunger, actually invaded the village of Lubian in Zamora and brazenly patrolled the streets. The watch-dogs were quickly killed and eaten and the terrified housewives cowered back from the doorways as lean grey muzzles were thrust underneath. Corrals were invaded nightly and once the dogs were dead there was no hope for the horses and cattle.

The mountain ranges to the north of Zamora hold many wolves, and every year hunts are organized to destroy them, but only with limited success. Rewards are offered as in France to those who bag the highest numbers, but the area is so remote that the wolves continue to breed and flourish despite all efforts to deal with them.

Across the border in Portugal wolves are still found, and during recent winters they have caused many losses among poultry and sheep. But here again the mountains are high and inaccessible, and the forests dense and thick, while the wolves have many escape routes to Spain. A recent visitor to the frontier district, Colonel Butt, was informed by the local inhabitants that wolves were a great nuisance, particularly in the winter when they moved down to the villages and attacked the livestock, though no instances of attacks upon human beings were reported.*

In Turkey wolves are relatively common. But this is perhaps only to be expected in a country so wild that even the presence of leopards is tolerated. Both wolves and bears patrol the no-man's-land on the frontiers of the Soviet Union and, undeterred by the savage watch-dogs, roam round the Kirghiz tents at night. There they are regarded as part of the background and no serious attempts at extermination have ever been undertaken. The same attitude to wolves prevails in Kurdistan, Turkestan and the steppes further east. There wolves are so plentiful and the areas so vast that no formal control is possible. So the beasts proliferate throughout Asia as far as China and, until recently, a small race survived in Japan. Further south the wolf occurs throughout Persia, Syria, Palestine, Arabia, Afghanistan and India, though the Indian wolf is a smaller and far less formidable creature than its northern cousin.

In Tibet wolves are heavily coated to withstand the rigorous climate. There the villages are protected by perhaps the most formidable breed of mastiffs in the world, and the wolves are of a corresponding rarity. Members of a recent

* It was reported from Lisbon on 4th February 1963 that the heaviest snowfalls for twenty-five years had brought foraging wolf packs into the valleys.

Mount Everest expedition were intrigued one day by the nervous bunching of a flock of sheep, until they realized that they were being followed by two large dogs. At least the beasts looked like dogs from a distance, but on closer inspection proved to be wolves. But probably ibex and Marco Polo sheep constitute the wolves' staple diet in Tibet as caribou do in Canada.

Apart from a pack which crossed the ice to an island in Lake Superior, wolves are supposed to be extinct in the United States of America. It is true that there are occasional invasions from Canada and Mexico, but in general only the wolf's small cousin, the coyote, remains to worry the farmers. The latter is as great a menace to poultry as the fox in Britain, and is also a dangerous spreader of rabies, but it is as harmless to man as the timber wolf is reputed to have been in the days when it was common. This seems very strange in the face of the comparative frequency of attacks on men by wolves in Europe, yet it seems that no instances have been recorded. Possibly the wolf was wiped out before it could grow familiar with men in America, or possibly it rarely bothered him as there were always plenty of bison, wapiti and caribou to eat.

In Scandinavia the status of the wolf is somewhat uncertain. In Finland the beast is outlawed, but the country is always open to invasion from Russia and in winter influxes occur. In Norway the wolf is common only in Lapland where it lives on reindeer and is hunted for its fur. In Sweden again it occurs in small numbers though with systematic hunting it is becoming progressively rarer. The chances are that it will hold its own for many years to come, and be even encouraged to survive in specially preserved areas.

Packs of wolves were observed near Moscow after the German retreat, and during 1963 a large "dog" was seen by some workmen wandering about a housing-estate in the same city. When they approached it it jumped from an upstairs window and was instantly killed by the fall. It proved to their amazement to be a wolf boldly on the prowl in the capital itself! So the savage enemy which menaced man long before the Ice Ages still lurks within sight of some of his most famous cities. Only disaster is required to increase its numbers, for in times of war and famine the wolf moves in. Should civilization end by nuclear fission then one thing is reasonably certain. About the ruined towns of Europe grey shapes will gather, though none may be alive to raise the cry "Wolf!"

# ADDENDA

Wolves have been much in the news since this book was written. It was reported in the press in 1984 that Russia was suffering from a plague of wolves. This may hardly have seemed like news, because if you mention wolves most people think of Russia. In fact there has long been a policy of extermination throughout the USSR and it wasn't until recently that experts suggested that wolves constituted the most natural way of controlling elk and deer. So the wolf population grew, livestock suffered and the authorities had second thoughts.

Attempts to preserve the wolf in Scandinavia also failed, though more leniency has been shown in Finland. The suggestion that wolves should be protected in Spain was howled down by farmers, the point being that wolves have much increased in the north-west of the country where the human population has shown a corresponding decrease. Despite this there is a sympathetic conservation lobby, whose claims were recently advanced on Channel 4. Erik Zimen investigated the wolf population in central Italy, but found nothing resembling an explosion. Marauding packs were occasionally seen, notably near l'Aquila, some sixty miles east of Rome, and some damage was suffered by flocks and foals. But the local population was often as unaware of the wolf's presence in their midst as city dwellers in Britain often are of that of foxes raiding their dust-bins.

Reports of attacks on human beings continue to come in. Eastern Turkey apparently suffers most, though a new breed of wolf-dog is proving successful. Reuters reported in 1987 that wolf packs were menacing villagers during the hard winter, while survivors of an earthquake were also attacked. A like fate befell villagers in Iran some years earlier. More incredible was an account of how a youth in Bosnia, who had lost his key, took refuge in an outhouse belonging to the farm and did battle with three wolves in succession. The first he beat to death with a flail, the second he throttled while the third he also killed. It seems that they were young wolves, sufficiently maddened by hunger to attack a sleeping man.

The myth that wolves react to music gained support from a report from Russia. In 1977 a wolf attacked some calves on a state farm near Minsk and was frightened off by a record of dogs howling. But the ruse failed to work and the wolf soon returned to continue its nefarious activities. However a record of a brass band playing a tango proved too much for its sensibilities. Squatting on its haunches it emitted mournful cries, as if hypnotized by the music and was easily captured when a coat was thrown over it. It was subsequently despatched to Leningrad Zoo.

A serious project to reintroduce wolves into Britain was put forward in 1986. The place selected for the experiment was the island of Rhum in the Scottish Hebrides, where a party of conservationists have been at work for several years and been busy among other things in reintroducing the sea-eagle. Since the large numbers of deer resident in the island suffer perforce an annual cull it was thought, as in Russia, that wolves might perform the task more efficiently, as well as replacing an interesting lost fauna. On the other side it was argued that the island is popular with tourists, while the conservationists have their families with them, including small children. The tale of Red Riding Hood dies hard.

Nevertheless wolves have been reintroduced to several wildlife parks and notably to the one at Dunachton in Inverness-shire, in the shadow of the Monadhliath mountains, where the last wolf in Scotland was killed as recently as 1743.

But even wildlife parks have their hazards, as was alarmingly demonstrated when members of the Animal

Liberation Army released a wolf from Cumbernauld, near Glasgow. It duly accounted for a brace of sheep before it was recaptured.

As for werewolves, the American *Sunday World* carried a story in 1979 of how a certain reverend gentleman had exorcized a man behaving like a wolf, when more authentic methods had failed. Moreover the claim was vouched for by an Anglican bishop, who had included it in a book about the devil! Still more amazing was a report of a wolf-child in Maine in 1975.

There seems little doubt that many, if not most, tales about wolves attacking human beings are exaggerated or embroidered, since they make such good copy for journalists who are unfamiliar with the beasts' habits. That wolves followed sleighs in Russia in hard winters is not to be doubted. But it was the horses they were pursuing, not the drivers. In France they were attracted by the scent of food and so followed up anyone carrying a basket. All this seems perfectly logical. Other tales are not so. The sensational tale about the Italian postman, with which this book opens, has since been discounted on the grounds that the man in question deliberately spread the tale to cover his disappearance when involved in a divorce case. Where the truth lies nobody knows.

Wolves, by their very nature, have a constant eye to the main chance and the story of the attack on the sleeping youth may well be basically true. Again peasants in Turkey, collapsed in the snow, might prove irresistible to a hungry pack. Wolves will certainly devour the dead and some of the so-called victims may already have expired. It is usually difficult, if not impossible, to get at the facts, since the occurrences are, in the main, reported from remote areas. Whenever attacks on human beings have been investigated they have generally proved false. Attacks by rabid wolves are another matter, as the terrible accounts contained in this book have amply shown.

A plan to kill up to 1,200 wolves in Alberta, in an attempt to halt the decline in numbers of elk, moose and caribou, has been vigorously opposed by animal conservation associations, on the grounds that hunters, not wolves, are mainly responsible. I am grateful to Mr Gavin Cooper for drawing my attention to this recent (1990) report.

A pack, estimated at ten wolves, is reported (May 1990) as surviving in the thickly forested area of south-east Norway, despite the hostility of local farmers.

Bills have just been introduced in the United States Senate (22 May 1990), as well as in the House of Representatives, to permit the reintroduction of the wolf.

The interesting thing is that, despite efforts to eliminate it, the wolf is still with us and appears to be acquiring more and more friends. There is, indeed, an anti-traditional wolf view lobby which stolidly maintains that wolves are much misunderstood. But then its members' experiences are largely confined to tame wolves. Dealing with wolves in the wild, and preserving livestock against their assaults, is a very different affair. However all conservationists are agreed that it would be highly regrettable if wolves actually disappeared. After all, they are the direct ancestors of the domestic dog and as such are worthy of preservation and study.